Grace Moments

OCTOBER–DECEMBER 2024

TIME OF GRACE

Published by Straight Talk Books
P.O. Box 301, Milwaukee, WI 53201
800.661.3311 / timeofgrace.org

Copyright © 2024 Time of Grace Ministry

All rights reserved. This publication may not be copied, photocopied, reproduced, translated, or converted to any electronic or machine-readable form in whole or in part, except for brief quotations, without prior written approval from Time of Grace Ministry.

Unless otherwise indicated, Scripture is taken from THE HOLY BIBLE, NEW INTERNATIONAL VERSION®, NIV® Copyright © 1973, 1978, 1984, 2011 by Biblica, Inc.® Used by permission. All rights reserved worldwide.

Scripture quotations marked EHV are from the Holy Bible, Evangelical Heritage Version® (EHV®) © 2019 Wartburg Project, Inc. All rights reserved. Used by permission.

Scripture quotations marked ESV are taken from The Holy Bible, English Standard Version®. Text Edition: 2016. Copyright © 2001 by Crossway, a publishing ministry of Good News Publishers. All rights reserved.

Scripture quotations marked KJV are taken from the King James Version. Text is public domain.

Scripture quotations marked MSG are taken from *THE MESSAGE*, copyright © 1993, 2002, 2018 by Eugene H. Peterson. Used by permission of NavPress. All rights reserved. Represented by Tyndale House Publishers, Inc.

Scripture quotations marked NLT are taken from the *Holy Bible*, New Living Translation, copyright © 1996, 2004, 2015 by Tyndale House Foundation. Used by permission of Tyndale House Publishers, Inc., Carol Stream, Illinois 60188. All rights reserved.

Printed in the United States of America
ISBN: 978-1-949488-96-8

TIME OF GRACE *is a registered mark of Time of Grace Ministry.*

OCTOBER

"Salvation is found in no one else, for there is no other name under heaven given to mankind by which we must be saved."

ACTS 4:12

October 1

Jesus is like my mother-in-law
Mike Novotny

Over the past 25 years, I have come to know my mother-in-law as a devout, hardworking, reliable, and generous child of God. Also (she gave me permission to tell you this), I have learned that she is a walking spoiler alert! If she sees a great movie before you do, watch out! She has a hard time keeping the good news to herself.

Jesus is a lot like that. Instead of making us live with the suspense and the fear (Will I be good enough to go to heaven? Will modern culture sweep away true Christian faith?), Jesus tells us how the story of human history ends.

Will Christianity die? **"I will build my church, and the gates of Hades will not overcome it"** (Matthew 16:18).

Will evil win? **"And the devil, who deceived them, was thrown into the lake of burning sulfur, where the beast and the false prophet had been thrown"** (Revelation 20:10).

Will you be good enough to be with God? **"[God] has reconciled you by Christ's physical body through death to present you holy in his sight, without blemish and free from accusation"** (Colossians 1:22).

There is hard work to do, a good fight to be fought, and a faithful race to be run, but take a deep breath today and let Jesus spoil the ending of our story—God and his people will win!

October 2

5 things I love about Jesus
Mike Novotny

In Revelation 19, we get a glorious glimpse of Jesus and of five things I love most about him. John reports: **"I saw heaven standing open and there before me was a white horse, whose rider is called Faithful and True. . . . His eyes are like blazing fire, and on his head are many crowns. . . . He is dressed in a robe dipped in blood. . . . He treads the winepress of the fury of the wrath of God Almighty. On his robe and on his thigh he has this name written:** KING OF KINGS AND LORD OF LORDS**"** (verses 11-16).

First, he is faithful/true. What Jesus says, he does. If he said he loves and forgives you, he loves and forgives you. Second, he is all-knowing ("his eyes are like blazing fire"). All the evidence is before his eyes, which means he judges with justice. Third, he is authoritative. The embroidery on his robe and the ink on his thigh reads, "KING OF KINGS AND LORD OF LORDS," which means no one can depose, out rule, or outvote him. Fourth, Jesus is holy, carrying out God's wrath against sin, smashing sinners like crushed grapes in a winepress (so don't you dare stand before Jesus holding on to sin!). Finally, Jesus is loving. His robe is dipped in the blood he shed on the cross to take away our sins so we wouldn't be sinners in the hands of an angry God but children in the arms of a forgiving Father.

What a Jesus! What a Savior!

October 3

Knocked out by Jesus
Mike Novotny

Apparently, the end of the world will be a lot like the day Mike Tyson fought Marvis Frazier. In 1986 a young Mike Tyson fought the son of boxing legend Joe Frazier, and ABC's *Wide World of Sports* was eager to see if Marvis could knock out Iron Mike. But then the bell rang . . . and Marvis didn't win. In fact, I'm not sure he even threw a real punch. Tyson's meaty uppercut smashed into Frazier's face and knocked him unconscious. Referee Joe Cortez started to count to ten but decided it was over at five. The official bout lasted 30 seconds, the fastest knockout of Mike Tyson's career.

That's what will happen with Jesus. You might think the end of the world, when every evil force gathers to fight against Jesus, will be a nail-biting event, but you'd be wrong. Revelation 19 doesn't give us a blow-by-blow recap of that battle but instead simply says: **"But the beast was captured, and with it the false prophet who had performed the signs on its behalf. . . . The two of them were thrown alive into the fiery lake of burning sulfur. The rest were killed with the sword coming out of the mouth of the rider on the horse"** (verses 20,21). Oh. That's it? Our fiercest enemies will be KO'd by Jesus just like that.

The devil may be a powerful foe, stronger than you, but he is not stronger than Jesus. Cling to Christ, and your biggest spiritual enemies will be knocked out sooner than you think.

October 4

Our eager Savior
Mike Novotny

I recently realized that the Bible is the biggest spoiler of any book ever. Instead of making us live the tension of good vs. evil, our Father spoiled the ending of our story on the very first page where our problems began.

You might be familiar with the fall into sin, when Adam and Eve doubted God and ate the forbidden fruit (Genesis 3:1-7). But did you notice how long it took God to tell us how our battle vs. evil would end? God didn't wait 2,000 pages until the book of Revelation or 1,500 pages until the birth of Jesus. In fact, he didn't even wait a day!

On the same page where sin entered the world, God promised a Savior. Just verses after the fall, God looked Satan in the eye and said, **"He will crush your head"** (Genesis 3:15). The One Adam and Eve knew as "he" and the One the Old Testament saints called the Messiah is the One we know as Jesus. He came into the world, resisted every evil, and crushed the devil by dying on a cross.

The world is so messed up (the headlines, the heartaches), and we are so messed up (our struggles, our sins), but we know how the story ends. We don't have to hold our breath. We don't have to worry where things are going. We know who sits on the glorious throne and who is crushed and thrown into a lake of fire. Don't worry for a single second. In the end, Jesus (and his people) win!

October 5

Am I in the wrong place?
Linda Buxa

Mark Gubin is a photographer whose home and studio are directly on the flight path to runway 19 at Milwaukee's Mitchell Airport. In 1978 he was bored and decided to have some fun. He took white paint and painted WELCOME TO CLEVELAND in block letters on his roof. Since then, passengers see the welcome sign, ring the call button, and ask the flight attendant if they are landing in the right place.

This story amuses me, but I'm not amused when I end up where I don't want to go in real life. I like when life is smooth, and I can get frustrated and disheartened when detours change my plans. Then I remember what Proverbs 16:9 says: **"In their hearts humans plan their course, but the Lord establishes their steps."**

I have plans, goals, and wishes, but God knows what I need. Maybe he's protecting me from a decision that won't be healthy for me. Maybe he's allowing me to struggle so I can bless someone with compassion in the future. Maybe he's just telling me to wait because *later* will be better than *right now*.

Proverbs reminds me that my plans are often short-term and shortsighted. Ultimately, God's plan for me includes bringing him glory now and living with him forever eternally. So even while I wrestle with how my path might look now, I know he's far more invested in me seeing the WELCOME HOME painted on the roof of my place when the angels take me to be with him forever.

October 6

Raise your right hand
Dave Scharf

"Raise your right hand. Do you swear to the tell the truth, the whole truth, and nothing but the truth?" Why do we raise our right hands when testifying in court? Recently, a tour guide in Boston told me that it dates from the 17th century when there was no standardized method of keeping records. If someone were convicted, the offense was branded on their right hand: "T" for theft, "M" for murder, and so on. It was a way to check the character of the witness who was testifying.

Imagine standing before God in his courtroom. What brands would your hand be given, including for crimes of thought that are just as damning? What letters would reveal your true character? The Bible says, "[Jesus] **forgave us all our sins, having canceled the charge of our legal indebtedness, which stood against us and condemned us; he has taken it away, nailing it to the cross**" (Colossians 2:13,14). That charge that stood against you is the document that records your personal responsibilities for a debt. Do you hear what the Bible says? That piece of paper with your signature on it is nailed to the cross. Instead of "D" being branded on your hand for "debtor," Jesus took the nails in his hands on the cross. Now your hand is "brandless" because of Jesus. He has forgiven all your sins! Raise your right hand and praise him today!

October 7

Stand guard
Katrina Harrmann

Once, a huge Cooper's hawk swooped low over my backyard. I have a very tiny backyard, but I also have a tiny chihuahua... a snack-size animal for a large, hungry hawk.

I quickly scooped up my dog when I saw that hawk.

And for several weeks afterward, I made sure to accompany our small dog whenever he went out, standing guard over him and glaring angrily at the sky—waving my arms at any large bird that would dare to swoop close.

It's easy to be vigilant when we can SEE the danger physically, isn't it? It's easy to make an effort when the danger is sitting there, staring over the fence line with its sharp beak and razor claws.

But when it's not *physically* there, we quickly forget.

I think our reaction to Satan is often similar.

We can't necessarily see him prowling around our homes and lives *physically*. If we could, imagine how much more on guard we would be! And how much more dedicated to our faith walk!

I'm sure Satan probably prefers it this way. After all, he's so much more crafty and cunning to fight when we can't see him. Often, we completely forget he's there at all!

Instead, let us be vigilant. Let us stand guard constantly and live our lives in a way that does honor to our Father in heaven!

"Be alert and of sober mind. Your enemy the devil prowls around like a roaring lion looking for someone to devour" (1 Peter 5:8).

October 8

144,000 in heaven?
Mike Novotny

"Then I looked, and there before me was the Lamb, standing on Mount Zion, and with him 144,000 who had his name and his Father's name written on their foreheads" (Revelation 14:1). What does it mean that John saw 144,000 people with Jesus (the Lamb) in heaven? Is there a capacity limit for heaven? (If so, I'm not sure if I want to share my faith—they might take my spot!)

No, like much of Revelation, this is a symbolic number that offers Christians great hope. In Revelation, the number 12 often refers to God's people (there were 12 tribes in Old Testament Israel and 12 apostles in Jesus' New Testament church). And the numbers 10 and 1,000 often represent the complete, full, total of something. Therefore, 144,000 (12 x 12 x 1,000) means the entire church, all true children of God, what some call the holy Christian church.

That makes this verse really good news. Despite the "beasts" we battle here on earth (read Revelation 13), God will bless and keep every last one of his chosen people. There aren't 143,000 in heaven, as if the devil snatched a few from the mighty hand of Jesus. No, all God's people will be saved and kept safe from the evil one. Despite the pushback, the persecution, and the temptation, God will get his faithful followers through it all.

That includes you, child of God. The Lord who began a good work in you will carry it on to completion until the day when you stand with the Lamb in heaven!

October 9

No bait and switch here!
Clark Schultz

A recent commercial makes me giggle out loud, and not for the reason you might think. Here's how it goes: A couple is about to take a scenic photo using the timer feature on their phone. There is a beautiful backdrop of mountains. The couple gets in close and begins their pose, but right before the photo is taken, an eagle swoops in and snatches the camera. What ensues is a car chase through rugged terrain, rivers, hills, and rocks to regain control of the camera. If you are caught up in the scene, you may fail to notice the fine print on the bottom that reads, "Professional driver—do not attempt this stunt on your own." It's not even the couple doing the driving. Talk about a bait and switch!

The world is full of bait and switches, but I'm so thankful God's Word isn't. **"But these are written that you may believe that Jesus is the Messiah, the Son of God, and that by believing you may have life in his name"** (John 20:31). Long ago Adam and Eve, the first couple, lost more than a camera in the Garden of Eden. They lost perfection. Enter Jesus, who traveled the rugged terrain of Earth, taking on human form, to win salvation for us.

There's no fine print of work-righteousness to climb the hill of salvation. The final photo to be taken is us enjoying the beautiful backdrop of heaven with our Savior for eternity. Now that's a commercial I can't wait to see.

October 10

Sucker punched
Christine Wentzel

Receiving devasting, life-changing news about your health or someone you love can feel like a sucker punch. But you don't need to be beaten to death by it. Reach out to those in your Christian community. They will help you remember what lies ahead for those who believe in Jesus.

Allow your Christian family into your pain so they can comfort you in Jesus and lift you up in prayer. Yes, at times it might be awkward; reaching out for help isn't always easy. I must confess my first impulse is to go it alone. But I know that only makes me an easy target for the devil. Being honest with God's people about that tendency to hide from the world is also a good step forward to stay in the protection of God's pasture—a bulwark from the devil, who hates honesty and really hates God's presence.

If you've been hit by a low blow recently, there are those who want to pray for you, eager to talk to the heavenly Father about your pain and remind you of his words to you:

"Do not fear, for I am with you. Do not be overwhelmed, for I am your God. I will strengthen you. Yes, I will help you. I will uphold you with my righteous right hand" (Isaiah 41:10 EHV).

Those punches can't steal your hope and peace in Jesus. You've got God and Christian friends on your side.

October 11

Be our guest
Liz Schroeder

As we go into tech week for our daughter's school production of Disney's *Beauty and the Beast,* the song "Be Our Guest" is in heavy rotation. In the bridge, Lumiere the candelabra croons in a thick French accent about how unnerving it is for a servant who isn't doing the job of serving other people.

Lumiere is right on the money! It's discomforting not to be doing something you were designed to do. It's unsettling to be a teacher who's not teaching, a pastor who's not shepherding, an author who's not writing, or an engineer who's not boring the other guests at a dinner party. (Thankfully, my engineer husband has a sense of humor. ☺)

The body of Christ is counting on you to use your gifts for the common good. **"The eye cannot say to the hand, 'I don't need you!' And the head cannot say to the feet, 'I don't need you!' On the contrary, those parts of the body that seem to be weaker are indispensable. Now you are the body of Christ, and each one of you is a part of it"** (1 Corinthians 12:21,22,27).

You are an invaluable part of the body of Christ, so be our guest to sing, invent, compute, nurse, fix, create, and preach. Be our guest to develop your gifts through online courses, hands-on practice, and lots of trial and error. Be our guest to seek out a mentor who will use the gospel to encourage your gifts. We're all servants, so let's get serving!

October 12

Shine a light on the bad stuff
Matt Trotter

My friend and I have been talking about our temptations so we can hold each other accountable. Life can keep us down at times, and though we know what we ought to do, we don't always do it. Sometimes we know God's will and choose to sin, and sometimes we just wake up on the wrong side of the bed and can't get the mood right. Toward the back of the Bible are letters from Peter and John, people who knew Jesus. The letters can be tools to change the day, the moment, or the shame that may be upon us. Feeling down, I read about a mindset shift from the apostle John:

"God is light; in him there is no darkness at all. If we claim to have fellowship with him and yet walk in the darkness, we lie and do not live out the truth. But if we walk in the light, as he is in the light, we have fellowship with one another, and the blood of Jesus, his Son, purifies us from all sin" (1 John 1:5-7).

I like this. It reminds me not to wallow in the darkness of my mistakes and guilt. You too can remember God has given us a new life in the light of Jesus, and we can testify to his truth by shining a light on the darkness of sin and shame. Don't deny the power of Jesus by getting stuck in a negative outlook. Darkness is powerless against the light of Jesus.

October 13

I (heart) Holy Communion
Mike Novotny

When I was a kid, I wasn't too happy about Holy Communion. My mom, because she's awesome, took me to church every Sunday and, because she's really awesome, took me to McDonald's afterward. That meant after every *Amen*, I could eat processed sausage patties in Jesus' name. But a few Sundays each month, my church celebrated Communion, where people would shuffle up to the altar to chew and sip slowly and then shuffle back to their pews, and—maybe it was just my grade school concept of time—it took forever! Especially when church was full! Didn't these shuffling saints know I was *this close* to sausage?!

But I've changed my mind about Communion. Oh, it still takes time, especially when church is full, but I've come to love it. I love giving Communion to you. I love receiving Communion for me.

Here's why: **"The Lord Jesus, on the night he was betrayed, took bread, and when he had given thanks, he broke it and said, 'This is my body, which is for you; do this in remembrance of me.' In the same way, after supper he took the cup, saying, 'This cup is the new covenant in my blood; do this, whenever you drink it, in remembrance of me'"** (1 Corinthians 11:23-25). Meditate today on the phrases "my body," "for you," "new covenant," "remembrance of me."

If you do, I bet you will come to love Holy Communion as much as I do!

October 14

All the single ladies
Jason Nelson

A characteristic of my new community is the number of single ladies who bought homes here. Some are older, and some are young. Some are divorced, and some are widows. They come in different shapes, sizes, and colors. Some work from home, and some go to an office. One of them scares me. But the thing they all have in common is their fierce independence. They can take care of themselves. They are very cautious about letting some guy move in and jeopardize what they have worked hard to establish. I admire them all.

They are a subset in the rich pageant of our society. They present a challenge for the church in reaching out to them. Traditional church talk regarding what men can do and women can do will rub them the wrong way. I doubt that old-school ladies guilds would interest them. But emphasizing their freedom in Christ might. **"They suddenly recognize that God is a living, personal presence, not a piece of chiseled stone. And when God is personally present, a living Spirit, that old, constricting legislation is recognized as obsolete. We're free of it! All of us!"** (2 Corinthians 3:17 MSG).

All of us have been liberated by Jesus. We are independent agents of his love with his Spirit living in us. We are free to become our strongest selves, single or married, male or female. We are free to look out for ourselves and free to obligate ourselves to the welfare of others.

October 15

Your brain disagrees
Matt Ewart

It is quite difficult to trick your own brain, especially when it comes to what it thinks about who you are. For example:

You can't go to the gym one time and consider yourself a bodybuilder. Your brain knows better.

You can't write a few sentences and then decide you are an author. Your brain knows better.

You can't call yourself a mechanic because you watched a YouTube video on how to fix your car. Your brain knows better.

What about something much more important? Does your brain ever challenge the idea that you are a loved, forgiven child of God?

Your mind might be quick to point out all the things that are wrong with your life. If God loves you, why are there all these bad things?

Or your mind might be quick to remind you that your life doesn't reflect the identity of a child of God. Your thoughts, words, and actions suggest that you are somebody else. Somebody less holy.

And it's right. But what your mind tends to forget is that you are declared holy because of Jesus' life, not yours. Your mind should recall his perfect righteousness, not your own. So remind your mind that the foundation of your identity was established at Jesus' empty tomb. Then your mind will be in the right place.

"Set your minds on things above, not on earthly things. For you died, and your life is now hidden with Christ in God" (Colossians 3:2,3).

October 16

You are a mountain
Andrea Delwiche

Most of the time we picture God as *our* mountain, *our* rock of refuge. In Psalm 125, each one of us is an immovable mountain: **"Those who trust in the Lord,"** the psalmist says, **"are like Mount Zion, which cannot be shaken but endures forever"** (verse 1). Picture it: Family problems, health issues, doubts, and fears rain down, each one capable of causing an avalanche of anxiety and disruption of your peace. All this trouble, yet you see yourself standing firm.

When we have a relationship with the triune God, who is worthy of our trust, we will not be moved. How do we know our God is worthy of trust? The psalm again points the way for us. We can trust God because **"as the mountains surround Jerusalem, so the Lord surrounds his people both now and forevermore"** (verse 2). God is always working for our good.

While God's protection makes us like mighty mountains, our memory of God's protection can be like a crumbling sandcastle. We need to meditate on God's love and faithfulness continually. In Psalm 16, King David shares his habit of meditation: **"I keep my eyes always on the Lord. With him at my right hand, I will not be shaken"** (verse 8).

Spend time in prayer, and consider this picture of yourself as a mountain whose base is God and who is surrounded by a hedge of God's love. Where in the past has God encircled and protected you?

You are never alone. Never forgotten. You are always loved. Always embraced by God.

October 17

Why people in heaven are so happy
Mike Novotny

Have you ever gone to a funeral and heard that Uncle So-and-So is now playing golf in heaven? or fishing in heaven? or finally united with his golden retriever in heaven?

I don't know all the details of what eternity will be like, but I do know what the book of Revelation reveals about our forever future. John writes, **"And they sang a new song before the throne. . . . They follow the Lamb wherever he goes. . . . They are blameless"** (14:3-5). These few lines remind us of the big things happening right now in heaven.

First, everyone is exceedingly happy. They aren't pacing in boredom or pouting like heaven is a raw deal; they are singing before the throne of God, bursting with joy and gratitude.

Second, everyone is closely connected to Jesus. Wherever the Lamb goes, his people do too. Being in his presence is all they want, because nothing compares to seeing the face of God and delighting in his unconditional love.

Third, everyone is blameless. Every sin is gone. Every feeling of unworthiness is erased. Everything wrong we've ever done has been left behind, erased by the blood of the Lamb.

Apparently, all the blameless need for eternal blessing is to be with Jesus. The next time you're at a funeral and someone makes a comment about our hobbies in heaven, remember what makes heaven so heavenly—simply being with God.

October 18

Running faithfully
Ann Jahns

Are you a runner? My dad, in contrast, was a "jogger." Even calling him that was a bit of a stretch. He moved at such a shuffling pace up and down the road by our house that we jokingly bought him a sweatshirt with an orange triangle and the words "slow-moving vehicle" on the back. Sometimes he was gone so long that we had to look down the road to make sure he was returning.

When I look at the Christian life, it reminds me of my dad's long, sustained jogs—definitely more marathons than sprints. Our Christian race can't be sustained by short, infrequent bursts of spirituality; it requires everyday faithfulness. It involves the discipline of regularly filling ourselves up with God's Word and prayer and fellowship with other Christians.

The writer of the book of Hebrews encourages us, **"Let us run with perseverance the race marked out for us, fixing our eyes on Jesus, the pioneer and perfecter of faith"** (Hebrews 12:1,2). The author knew that our determination alone isn't enough to keep us sustained through this challenging marathon. Only focusing on our Savior will do that. It's only through faith in him, who ran the race perfectly in our place, that we can persevere.

Maybe we can all learn a lesson in perseverance from my dad. He didn't run fast, but he ran faithfully and without fail. With strength only found in God's Word, we too can keep putting one foot in front of the other faithfully with perseverance until the day we finish our race.

October 19

Two types of freedom
Andrea Delwiche

Are you desensitized to suffering? It's so easy to scroll through stories, shake our heads, and move on. Absorb these words from Psalm 129: **"They have greatly oppressed me from my youth . . . but they have not gained the victory over me. Plowmen have plowed my back and made their furrows long"** (verses 1-3). What a metaphor of suffering!

But read how the Lord brings relief: **"But the Lord is righteous; he has cut me free from the cords of the wicked"** (verse 4). How do we join with Jesus in cutting people free?

This task radiates through Scripture and in Jesus' own words and actions. We are called as followers of Christ to bring two types of freedom—the good news of freedom from sin and freedom from suffering. In both tasks, we are operating beyond our own capabilities. God alone gives salvation, and no one person can mitigate human suffering. We must work with God and others.

Look to Matthew 25:31-46 and see what Christ asks of us. He asks us to follow his example. There was no person whom he disdained to help. Imagine explaining to Jesus why we turned our backs on others because of fear, hatred, indifference, or busyness.

Listen to God's directive and promise: **"If you do away with the yoke of oppression, with the pointing finger and malicious talk, and if you spend yourselves in behalf of the hungry and satisfy the needs of the oppressed, then your light will rise in the darkness, and your night will become like the noonday"** (Isaiah 58:9,10).

October 20

Being recognized
Katrina Harrmann

Several years ago, we switched schools for our kids . . . my son was in fourth grade. Oh boy, was that stressful! I remember going to the fall open house ice cream social and not knowing a single other person there. I could practically see my kiddo wilt at the sight of all those kids who already knew each other, laughing and running and chasing each other on the playground.

And I couldn't "fix" it.

Just when I felt the bottom dropping out of my stomach, a little boy wandered up who had once played summer baseball with my son. And he asked my son if he wanted to throw a football.

The joy on my son's face at being recognized! All it took was one person to do that, and the rest of the day (and year!) were easy by comparison!

There's a big difference between being seen and being recognized.

Walk any major city street, and you can be seen by thousands but still be lonely.

But the minute someone spots you and their eyes light up because they KNOW you? WOW! What a powerful difference that makes!

Our heavenly Father sees AND recognizes us. He looks past the filth of our sin and looks us in the eye and says, "I KNOW you. You are MINE."

WOW! What a difference that makes—an *eternal* difference!

"Do not fear, for I have redeemed you; I have summoned you by name; you are mine" (Isaiah 43:1).

October 21

Truth over lies
Dave Scharf

Lying has consequences. There's a story about a father who wanted to teach his son the destructiveness of lying. He took a new board and pounded ten nails into it. He said, "This represents the lies you've told. I want you to fix each of the lies by pulling out the nails." The son did. Afterward, his father asked him, "Could you fix the lies?" The son said, "Well, the nails are gone, but the holes from the nails are still there." He got the point. Trust is destroyed. Feelings are hurt. Lives are changed. Relationships are strained or destroyed. Just think of how lies have affected your life.

What should you do? First John 1:9 says, **"If we confess our sins, he is faithful and just and will forgive us our sins and purify us from all unrighteousness."** The Bible does not say here, "He is faithful and loving," though it certainly could have. Instead, Jesus forgives you because he is "faithful and just." Jesus already paid for your sins on the cross. Therefore, it would be unjust to withhold forgiveness. That would be requiring a double payment since your sins have already been forgiven and paid for. So now what? Confess your sin if you are the one who has lied, knowing that Jesus has forgiven you. And if you are the one who has been lied to? Remember that Jesus paid for that sin. Do what he does with it. Forgive it.

October 22

A call for discernment
Jan Gompper

Have you heard someone say, "God spoke to me"—meaning they heard from God through direct revelation outside of reading the Bible?

Abraham, Moses, the prophets, Jesus, Saul/Paul, and John all heard from God directly. But in these instances, God chose to communicate directly in an audible way at crucial junctures in the history of salvation.

Since the salvation story was completed in the death and resurrection of Jesus and has been fully revealed to us in Scripture, there's no reason for God to give any "new revelations" today.

In a seminar entitled "A Call for Discernment," biblical theologian Justin Peters cautions against claims of directly hearing from God. Peters warns that although the Christian church has won the battle over God's Word being inerrant, we are still fighting the idea that the Word is sufficient.

He elaborates that because many Christians today focus on their *feelings* about God more than on their *knowledge* of God, they desire some sort of experience—a vision or "still small voice." But God doesn't urge us to grow in our feelings but rather to **"be transformed by the *renewal of [our minds]*, that by testing [we] may *discern* what is the will of God, what is good and acceptable and perfect"** (Romans 12:2 ESV).

As Peters puts it: *"If you want to hear from God, read your Bible. If you want to audibly hear from God, read your Bible out loud."**

---
* Justin Peters, "How to Hear God's Voice Today?" youtube.com, May 10, 2015, Video, 44:17, https://www.youtube.com/watch?v=JItLcIFL2F8.

October 23

Spend time at the tomb
Linda Buxa

At the Union Oyster House in Boston, you'll find John F. Kennedy's favorite table. At a supper club near my house, there's a money drop that was used by Al Capone and a booth known to be the mobster's table. When I visited the Vatican in college, our tour guide talked about the place where St. Peter is buried.

What is it about being at a place where famous people have been? Why are we so fascinated? Maybe it's because these places remind us that famous people were truly people—real people with real lives who needed to eat with their real friends.

Maybe that's why so many Christians say they spend time at the cross. Not Jesus' literal cross, but going back to the place, the moment, where we hear our real Savior who lived a real life say, "It is finished." At the cross we see that God punished Jesus in our place—and now we have a holy standing before God.

Mind if I suggest that maybe we should spend just as much (if not more) time at the empty tomb? That's where we see that God defeated death. That's where Jesus said Mary's name and turned her grief to joy. That's where we hear that because he's alive, we have eternal life too. Death has no sting, no power, no victory. Jesus wins—and so do we!

"He is not here; he has risen, just as he said. Come and see the place where he lay" (Matthew 28:6).

October 24

A better mansion awaits
Clark Schultz

My wife told me to take a hike, a 21-mile hike around Lake Geneva in Wisconsin to be exact. Her family loves to hike. I get tired spelling the word *hike*. Alas, it was a time to be together kid free for a day.

Walking, we saw the Wriggly Estates, Stone Manor, and Edgewood Estates—all beautiful lakefront properties. Even some of the less famous homes took our breath away. Conversations ensued about what a place like that would cost and which was our favorite "mansion." Each conversation ended with something like, "If we win the lottery . . ." or "Someday, maybe . . ."

I'm not sure what mile marker of life you're on, but Jesus tells us that each of us has a mansion already waiting for us: **"In my Father's house are many mansions: if it were not so, I would have told you. I go to prepare a place for you. And if I go and prepare a place for you, I will come again, and receive you unto myself; that where I am, there ye may be also"** (John 14:2,3 KJV). This is his gift to us by grace.

As we hiked around Lake Geneva, we noticed some homes that were run down and not maintained. Our heavenly mansion is not made with earthly materials, so it is **"an inheritance that can never perish, spoil or fade"** (1 Peter 1:4). So fellow hikers, enjoy the walk, take in the sights, and when you see a mansion, know that an even better one awaits.

October 25

There's always something . . .
Mike Novotny

There's always something that did, does, or will go wrong, isn't there? Just when you finally fix this, then that happens. Maybe you're killing it at work, but your friends are frustrated that you aren't around like you used to be. So you spend more time with your friends, but then the boss is frustrated you don't do what you used to do. Maybe you're a mom who never feels caught up. Or a dad who can't figure out how to win at work and at home. Or maybe work and home are finally good, but then the doctor tells you something bad. The curse of this earth is that there's always something that can go wrong, did go wrong, or might go wrong tomorrow.

That's why we need a place where there's never something to worry about. Never something to feel bad about. Never something to fix. Never something we wish we had. Never something that went wrong or might go wrong. Never something that keeps us up at night or overwhelms us during the day.

Which is exactly what God promised us at the end of the Bible! **"I saw the Holy City, the new Jerusalem, coming down out of heaven from God, prepared as a bride beautifully dressed for her husband. . . . 'There will be no more death or mourning or crying or pain, for the old order of things has passed away'"** (Revelation 21:2,4).

There will always be something until the day when Jesus returns. Then there will only be something good.

October 26

Sons, not slaves
Daron Lindemann

Jesus told a parable about a father and two of his sons (Luke 15). Both sons believed it was by performance that they earned a place in their father's heart and household.

"Make me like one of your hired servants" (verse 19) was the reinstatement plan of the younger son. He had run away with his father's money but now wanted to return!

"All these years I've been slaving for you and never disobeyed your orders" (verse 29) was the older son's self-justification for pouting. He became upset when his father actually welcomed his little brother home.

The father interrupted the younger son's explanation of his plan, ordered lavish gifts, and called him **"this son of mine"** (verse 24).

To the older son, lost without ever leaving home, the father encouraged, **"Son . . . you are always with me, and everything I have is yours"** (verse 31).

These young men thought they needed to be slaves and servants for their father to accept them. But he loved each of them as his "son." When they wondered, "Can we ever do enough?" he loved them with forgiveness and let them live in faith and freedom.

God's grace does not allow you to find your identity, purpose, or success as a hired servant or coerced slave for your heavenly Father. You still work, but as a privileged son!

Free. Lavished with gifts. Unconditionally loved. Always welcomed.

Who is trying to please you by their performance? Love them the same way.

October 27

Perfection made complete
Christine Wentzel

"Son though he was, he learned obedience from what he suffered and, once made perfect, he became the source of eternal salvation for all who obey him" (Hebrews 5:8,9).

Wasn't Jesus already perfect? This was my question during a church service one evening. I leaned in for an answer because I know that Jesus, the Son of God, is perfect, but a casual reading of these verses may seem contradictory.

Here's what I learned: On another evening over two thousand years ago, our Redeemer was in a garden called Gethsemane praying to his Father in heaven. He was in agony over his *final act of perfect obedience* to be the Lamb of God who takes away the sin of the world. Jesus alone lived a life without sin. He took on the sin of the world by giving up his life as a punishment for us.

In that garden just before Jesus' crucifixion, he offered another example of Christian living for his disciples both then and now. The lesson was about what obedience to our Father-God looks like. It's not always easy.

When we walk in obedience, the devil will tempt us to stop. Don't listen! Instead remember the selfless sacrifice Jesus fulfilled on the cross in our place, separated from God the Father because Jesus carried and became our sin. Jesus knew this was coming as he prayed in such sorrow and trouble in the Garden of Gethsemane.

"It is finished!" Jesus said from the cross (John 19:30). Perfection made complete.

October 28

The entire Bible in 4 words
Mike Novotny

You can summarize the 700,000+ words of the Bible with four key words.

First, *creation*. **"In the beginning God created the heavens and the earth,"** and it was good (Genesis 1:1). God spoke, and stars, mountains, and people were created, and it was very good. But that paradise only lasted for 2 pages.

Because then came *rebellion*. The devil, a rebellious angel, urged Adam and Eve to follow his example. "Don't!" God had said. But they did. "Follow my truth," God had urged. But they followed their own. And the curse came into the earth like a nuclear bomb. Labor pains, thorns, death, doubting God, and disbelieving his truth became the new normal.

But God responded with *salvation*. God loved those rebels so much that he promised to fix what their sin had broken, to send a Savior to crush the devil and save them and us from what we deserved. And it took a "few" pages (a.k.a. the entire Old Testament), but that salvation came in Jesus. Thank God it did!

But we still ache for more, don't we? For bodies that don't hurt. For relationships that aren't strained. For a world without tornados and floods. That's why the Bible ends with *restoration*. God has promised that one day Jesus will return in glory and there will be a whole new world, a place where our bodies will be made glorious and new, without torn ligaments or anxious thoughts or bad backs, where we will walk with God in perfect happiness.

Creation. Rebellion. Salvation. Restoration. That's the entire Bible in just four words.

October 29

An encouraging word
Jan Gompper

If I could have a do-over in my teaching career, I would encourage my students more. I taught college theater for most of my career and often focused too much on how my students could improve, not always giving them the accolades they also needed to hear.

Being an encourager doesn't come naturally. Satan wants nothing more than for us to tear each other down rather than build each other up. Sinful pride, jealousy, and insecurities can prevent us from uttering encouraging words to someone else. If we haven't been the recipient of much encouragement, we may also have a harder time doling it out.

Thankfully, God understands that there might be an "encouragement deficit" in the human condition. That's why he frequently encourages us to encourage others:

- "But encourage one another daily, as long as it is called 'Today,' so that none of you may be hardened by sin's deceitfulness" (Hebrews 3:13).
- "Therefore encourage one another and build each other up" (1 Thessalonians 5:11).

But God doesn't expect us to go it alone. He sends his Holy Spirit to encourage us in our spiritual journeys and to teach us how to encourage others. Before Jesus ascended to heaven, he told his disciples, **"I will ask the Father, and he will give you another advocate** [encourager] **to help you and be with you forever"** (John 14:16).

"May the God who gives endurance and encouragement give you the same attitude of mind toward each other that Christ Jesus had" (Romans 15:5).

October 30

Two key ingredients
Jason Nelson

I spent part of my ministry as a church consultant. I tried to help churches grow. I was invited to churches that wanted to grow because many churches weren't growing. We used a sophisticated process that included community and congregational analyses, questionnaires, and interviews. We provided reports of our findings and made ministry recommendations based on our research. Some churches implemented them with good results.

My son has been a member of a number of churches. He's not a consultant, but he has his own take on what is required to have a growing church. He thinks there are two key ingredients. I would like to pose his observations as questions.

Is the pastor the kind of person people want to be around?
Is the building the kind of place people want to be in?

There is room for lively discussion in responding to his questions. But I think he nailed it. His simple answer to both is . . . lighten up. Be bright! That is a tangible way to be what Jesus told us we are: **"You are the light of the world"** (Matthew 5:14). Who wouldn't want to be around a bright pastor in a bright space with a bright message surrounded by other bright people?

Let's stipulate that it all depends on the power of the gospel and work of the Holy Spirit. Let's dismiss the "yeah buts" of change resisters. And let's accept that there are factors under our control that make a difference.

October 31

Hey there, little rowboat
Matt Trotter

When I was becoming a believer in Jesus, I struggled to understand the concept of the moment of being saved. Apparently, I'm not alone, because I learned we Christians can and should be thoughtful about how redemption happens. Is it a choice? acceptance? work? belief? I asked anyone who would listen, "What must I do to be saved?"

So did some people who lived by the sea in Jesus' day, and some of those people were fisherman. The Bible scholars who taught those fishermen whined to Jesus about his claims on the shores of Galilee, and Jesus said, **"Stop grumbling among yourselves. . . . No one can come to me unless the Father who sent me draws them, and I will raise them up at the last day"** (John 6:43,44).

The first 44 times I read that, I skipped right past the verb ("draws") to the victory party ("raise them up at the last day"). Some Bible scholars view that metaphorically: God draws your consciousness to think about him.

But I think this teaching draws a really beautiful fisherman's picture of how we are saved. The Greek word used for "draws" in that instance is also "to draw/drag a boat across sand." I don't know how many times you've tried to draw a boat across sand, but good luck. It's a one-sided tug-of-war between the guy pulling the rope and dead weight.

Point made, Greek language! We are dead weight like a fisherman's boat. No one can come to Jesus unless God drags them. God is dragging you to him now. Believe it.

NOVEMBER

"For where your treasure is,
there your heart will be also."

MATTHEW 6:21

November 1

The generation in between
Ann Jahns

Have you heard the term "sandwich generation"? Are you a card-carrying member? You are if you are "sandwiched" between two generations—your children and your aging parents—and are caring for them both.

The sandwich generation is a place of special blessings . . . and some burdens. It's a place of frantically doing a wellness check on your octogenarian dad because he lives alone and isn't answering his phone. It's a place of keeping your toddler granddaughter overnight so her exhausted parents get a break. It's a place of driving hours to pick up your young adult son on the side of the road because his car broke down. All on the same weekend. And let's face it—you're not that young anymore, and your energy levels aren't what they used to be.

Then Monday comes, and you head back to work, depleted. But this coming weekend, you'd do it all again, because you love them all so much.

Do you ever wonder why God is giving you these special blessings and burdens? Perhaps he gives you these opportunities so you can tap into deep wells of compassion you never knew you had—and through that you fulfill your calling by loving others. **"Let us not become weary in doing good,"** encourages the apostle Paul, **"for at the proper time we will reap a harvest if we do not give up"** (Galatians 6:9).

I know you're weary, friend. But don't give up. God will graciously continue to replenish your well of compassion and will bless you as you bless others.

November 2

A positive review for God

Daron Lindemann

The sign at my chiropractor reads, "Give us a positive review on Yelp and Google. Show us, and receive 15% off your next visit."

Businesses thrive on more customers. Positive reviews can help. God wants positive reviews too, but for an additional reason. Your positive review of God is good for you.

Psalm 117 (the shortest chapter of the Bible) says, **"Praise the Lord, all you nations; extol him, all you peoples. For great is his love toward us, and the faithfulness of the Lord endures forever. Praise the Lord."**

The first and last words of the psalm serve as bookends, embracing the main message: "Praise the Lord." When your thoughts begin and end with God . . . when your day begins and ends with God . . . when your priorities begin and end with God . . . then everything else in between will be in its proper place in your life.

Praise means to cheer. A stronger synonym, *extol*, is making exuberant statements about the greatness of something. Why gush about God? Notice that little word *for* in the middle of the psalm. Exuberance about God means you're excited about him and his love more than anything else.

Where is that love of God targeted? "Toward us," not just floating around as positive energy.

Did you know? Not only is Psalm 117 the shortest chapter of the Bible; it is also the middle chapter. The center. The bull's-eye. It's all about this: the great love of God and your positive review of praise.

November 3

House of reputations
Katrina Harrmann

When my oldest son was just nine years old, I was helping him study for a social studies test.

As I was quizzing him, I asked, "What two bodies make up the legislature?"

He promptly answered, "The Senate and the House of Reputations."

I got a good laugh out of that. Because, oh my, all those colorful reputations! These days, you can hardly turn on your television or switch on your computer without seeing interesting stories about the antics of our politicians. Their reputations are indeed on full and vivid display.

November makes many people think of politics, whether they want to or not. Election time often gets people riled up as they argue for or against whatever policy or politician they support.

But it's important to remember to keep it in perspective. While God gives us politicians to help lead our nation—from whatever party they may happen to be—HE is the one who holds everything in his hands.

Respect our leaders? Yes. Jesus said, **"Give back to Caesar what is Caesar's"** (Matthew 22:21). And even more, *PRAY* for them! (Oof, this is not always easy, is it?)

But in the end? Rest easy knowing that God is Lord of all. And try to get along peaceably with one another, even with our myriad of different opinions on the subject of politics.

"Let everyone be subject to the governing authorities, for there is no authority except that which God has established. The authorities that exist have been established by God" (Romans 13:1).

November 4

Accept trouble
Matt Trotter

I collect bikes. My wife and mother both roll their eyes at the pedal-powered fleet. Today I sought to pull my SUV into our garage and not crush my bikes. I missed the bikes and scraped my SUV. I was angry at myself.

This made me think of the righteous man Job after his wife encouraged him to blame God. **"He replied, 'You are talking like a foolish woman. Shall we accept good from God, and not trouble?'"** (Job 2:10).

Job was right to question his wife. My wife's skepticism of my fleet of bikes is quite different than Mrs. Job, who had lost her whole family and more. Job's question is a good technique to reduce the temperature of our rage.

- When we scrape the paint off our car, should we accept good from God and not trouble?
- When a friend confides his addiction, should we accept good from God and not trouble?
- When a country invades another, should we accept good from God and not trouble?
- When I get a cold from the guy on the airplane, should I accept good from God and not trouble?

Much will come and go in this world, and the pain and trouble will tempt us to anger. Yet as promised to believers in Rome centuries after Job, **"We know that in all things God works for the good of those who love him, who have been called according to his purpose"** (Romans 8:28). Let's not blame but trust in God. No pain matters compared to keeping the faith in the Father, Son, and Holy Spirit.

November 5

Scared of Satan?
Mike Novotny

Are you scared of Satan? For all of human history, Satan has been deceiving people into all kinds of sin. If you're a compassionate person, he'll tempt you to be a people pleaser who always says yes, who burns out by ignoring your created limits. If you're a driven person, he'll drive you to forget about others' emotions, opinions, and goals. If you're good with words, he'll make you great at arguing. If you're good with money, he'll fixate your faith on the bottom line. Satan knows what works with you.

Are you scared of Satan? John's Revelation offers us a wake-up call and a way out: **"The dragon [Satan] stood in front of the woman who was about to give birth, so that it might devour her child the moment he was born. . . . And her child was snatched up to God and to his throne. The woman fled into the wilderness to a place prepared for her by God"** (12:4-6). The vivid imagery reminds us that we are no match for Satan (infants and postpartum moms aren't the best at battling dragons), yet by God's intervention, the dragon doesn't win.

This symbolic picture reveals to us that God is stronger than Satan. And since God saves and protects his people through the truth of the gospel, you will be okay. Let Satan breathe the fire of his accusations and try to convince you that evil will get the last word. Because of Jesus, he can't devour you. Not today. Not ever.

Amen!

November 6

He will watch with us
Jan Gompper

"Then he returned to the disciples and found them asleep. He said to Peter, 'Couldn't you watch with me even one hour?'" (Matthew 26:40 NLT).

Have you ever read this verse and thought, "How terrible of Peter, James, and John! How could they have not honored Jesus' request to watch with him while he went into Gethsemane to pray? I'd have stayed awake!"

Really? I often can't "watch with Jesus" for 15 minutes. While listening to a pastor's message on Sunday, saying my daily prayers, reading a devotion (or even writing one), my focus on Jesus is often pulled in other directions. Too easily daily concerns dart in and out of my brain, robbing me of the quality time I desire to have with my Lord.

And Satan does a victory dance whenever this happens because the last thing he wants me (or you) to do is "watch with Jesus." The more he can distract us from what's most needed in our lives, the more he thinks he can eventually pull us away from Jesus altogether.

But what Satan always forgets is how faithful Jesus is. He not only forgave his sleepy, fearful disciples; he commissioned them, promising that he would always watch with them: **"Be sure of this: I am with you always, even to the end of the age"** (Matthew 28:20 NLT).

And when we struggle to watch with Jesus, or even if we sometimes run from him or betray him, we have this same promise.

November 7

From barren to harvest
Andrea Delwiche

Are you in a struggle that makes it hard to imagine sowing seeds of joy? Yes, you have had times of goodness, but now . . . does joy feel impossible? Sometimes it's a struggle to *locate* the seeds of joy, much less prepare the soil and plant them. These are the shadow times. We need someone to witness to us that green leaves and sun-ripened tomatoes (or joy) will come again.

Psalm 126 can provide that service. It begins by recalling a promise fulfilled by God: **"When the Lord restored the fortunes of Zion, we were like those who dreamed. Our mouths were filled with laughter, our tongues with songs of joy. . . . The Lord has done great things for us, and we are filled with joy"** (verses 1-3).

One minute we fly with joy, and the next we crash back down, having forgotten the goodness we so recently celebrated. Our emotions are like dandelion seeds, blown by every breeze.

But here the psalmist holds out a sign of new growth where all seems dead: **"Those who go out with weeping, carrying seed to sow, will return with songs of joy, carrying sheaves with them"** (verse 6). Goodness will emerge from the barren ground. Growth takes time, but with water, nutrients, and sunshine, your harvest will be realized.

Our God is the Lord of the harvest. Growth and greenness out of scorched or parched earth is his specialty.

Ask him to steady your hand as you plant. He will guard your heart and mind to anticipate a harvest of joy.

November 8

Everybody's weird but us
Jason Nelson

And I'm not so sure about you. Isn't that what we think sometimes? Especially after a trip to Walmart. I mean, after we get past the polite first impressions of being on our best behavior and get to know each other, we find out we are all weirdos. We all have idiosyncrasies that could alienate others. If you spend enough time with someone, you will realize they are a little off in some way. The question is, will we love them anyway, even if they make us uncomfortable?

I don't think Jesus would shop exclusively at Macy's just to be with a "better class" of people. I think Jesus would be quite comfortable at Walmart or any other gathering place of diverse people because he came to redeem this freak show we call humanity. He once told a prominent Pharisee who invited him for lunch: **"The next time you put on a dinner, don't just invite your friends and family and rich neighbors, the kind of people who will return the favor. Invite some people who never get invited out, the misfits from the wrong side of the tracks. You'll be—and experience—a blessing. They won't be able to return the favor, but the favor will be returned—oh, how it will be returned!—at the resurrection of God's people"** (Luke 14:12-14 MSG).

The invitation to the great banquet of the Lamb of God is extended to all, including weirdos like you and me.

November 9

Turning to Jesus
Matt Trotter

I have an idol problem. See if you can guess what it is. Each day I jump out of bed thinking I've got to improve everything right now. I want to fix the world. Here are my top six problems today: 1) everyone needs faith in Jesus, 2) injustice, 3) yesterday, 4) politics, 5) work, 6) snooze button.

Realistically, I can't do much about any of it. So in an effort to improve, I read the Bible, looking for tips and wisdom from books like James and Proverbs, which are excellent sources. But somehow I still wake up edgy about the situations I see and feel, things done and not done.

For an antidote, I can only look to one place. I turn from my problems to look for God's gospel encouragement: **"They tell how you *turned to God* from idols to serve the living and true God, and to wait for his Son from heaven, whom he raised from the dead—Jesus, who rescues us from the coming wrath"** (1 Thessalonians 1:9,10).

Have you figured out what my idol problem is? Every day I wake up . . . angry. The problems are too big for a human to solve. And perhaps by the Creator's design, the problems I perceive won't reduce for the present age.

Tomorrow there will be about six more things that I dream to fix before breakfast. I'd be better off starting my day by turning to Jesus.

November 10

So long, earthly body
Liz Schroeder

"Meth and alcohol were my two best friends. I didn't need anyone else." Although Gloria had left that life behind, it had taken a toll on her body. She told our support group that an oral surgeon was going to pull 15 of her teeth that had decayed from drug use and neglect. "What man is going to want me now?" she asked as she grabbed a tissue. "Not that I care," she added without much conviction.

As God would have it, the lesson for that night was on our heavenly bodies. We read Paul's words together: **"The body that is sown is perishable, it is raised imperishable; it is sown in dishonor, it is raised in glory; it is sown in weakness, it is raised in power; it is sown a natural body, it is raised a spiritual body"** (1 Corinthians 15:42-44).

It took zero effort to convince the ladies in the group that their bodies were weak, perishable, and had been dishonored. Even if you haven't abused substances, you feel it too, don't you? When an old sports injury keeps you from exercising, when you can't eat the foods you used to enjoy, or when you research how much it would cost to cover up a tattoo you now regret.

Later that week, I brought Gloria a smoothie and a word of comfort. That's what makes a gospel-centered recovery program so practical and effective. What man will want you now? Jesus. Who is a true friend? Jesus. How will you be raised to life with a glorious body? Only through Jesus.

November 11

Conquerors vs. more than conquerors
Karen Spiegelberg

What does it mean to be a conqueror? One definition is, "One who overcomes." I'm sure you can think of things you've overcome or conquered. My most memorable conquest (besides childbirth!) was climbing Pike's Peak in Colorado via the Barr Trail. For a flatlander from Wisconsin, it was no easy feat. The trail starts at 7,500 ft. above sea level. Then for 13 miles, it climbs to over 14,000 ft. The climb sucks the air out of you because of the altitude and elevation change. The view from the top is indescribable though and worth the journey.

What does it mean to be *more than* a conqueror? Human brains can't even process that. In Romans 8:37, the apostle Paul assured the Romans and us that all kinds of things would be thrown at us and challenge our faith. He said, **"In all these things we are more than conquerors through him who loved us."** To be more than a conqueror means that prior to even having a problem or something to overcome, we *can* overcome it through Christ. Before health, work, family, or other struggles come our way, he has already conquered it all, and there is nothing that he can't conquer because of his love and presence within us. We are more than conquerors through him!

When we understand who we are in Christ and what he's done for us, how beautiful it is. More beautiful than any view from the top of a mountain!

Tune up
Matt Ewart

"Since we live by the Spirit, let us keep in step with the Spirit" (Galatians 5:25).

I have an old piano that sits in my house. When I say "old," I don't mean it's an expensive antique. It's just old and worn out. Someday we will have to pay someone to take it from our house.

Another instrument that sits in my house is a guitar that's just as old as the piano. Thankfully it's light enough that I won't have to pay someone to haul it away.

What these two instruments have in common is that they are perfectly in tune. At least they are in tune with each other. A C chord on the guitar will perfectly match up with a C chord on the piano.

The problem with these two instruments is that they are *only* in tune with each other. The piano is several notes flat because it is unable to be tuned. The guitar is tuned down to match the piano.

It's easy to follow that same path in life. Over time, our hearts naturally get "tuned down" to the level of our wants and our desires. And it's easy to miss if we are only in the company of people who are tuned down similarly.

Keep in tune today. Ask the Spirit to enlighten your heart with his truth. It's okay if the world thinks you sound different. God will tune your heart to sing his praise.

November 13

When life is suddenly scary
Mike Novotny

One of my friends once went from attending Bible study to facing serious prison time, all in the course of a single day. On Thursday, he was absorbing God's Word, but a day later, he was arrested and facing a scary sentence despite his claims of innocence.

Has life ever gotten suddenly scary for you? Without warning, the landlord raises the rent, the manager cuts back your hours, the medical bill arrives, or the mechanic calls and says, "Are you sitting down?" Out of the blue, you find a lump you never noticed before, something snaps in your knee, or the doctor drops the c-word—*cancer*. On an otherwise sunny day, your parents sit you down and say, "Divorce," your only friend from work tells you she's transferring, or you lose someone you really love. When scary and sudden overlap, it feels like you can't not be afraid.

But those suddenly scary moments are when Jesus is at his best. During a terrifying storm, **"[Jesus] replied, 'You of little faith, why are you so afraid?' Then he got up and rebuked the winds and the waves, and it was completely calm"** (Matthew 8:26). Jesus wants to save you from small faith by giving you powerful proof of how much he can do and how much he cares about you.

Remember who Jesus is—your powerful King, your compassionate Savior, your loving and risen Redeemer—and your faith will have a good reason to be completely calm during the next storm in your life.

November 14

Nothing could be more perfect
Dave Scharf

Recently, I attended a worship service that seemed doomed from the start. The pastor introduced the service and pointed to the screen that would guide the service. Just then the screen showed an error message and retracted to show a blank wall. The pastor hadn't noticed, so the organist tried to get his attention from the balcony to no avail. The pastor began speaking, but his microphone crackled more than Rice Krispies, forcing the pastor to switch to the handheld mic to conduct a baptism. The family formed a line around the font, but as the pastor began speaking, the little boy who was soon to be baptized ran away from the font with his father chasing after him. What a mess! Nothing more could have gone wrong. But then . . .

Nothing could have been more perfect. Titus 3:5 says, **"He saved us, not because of righteous things we had done, but because of his mercy. He saved us through the washing of rebirth and renewal by the Holy Spirit."** I watched as the entire family, not just the restless little boy, was baptized. What a beautiful picture of what our Savior does for all of us. He came into this messy, sinful world to save us by his cross. He comes into the mess of our lives to save us through Baptism, that washing of rebirth and renewal by the Holy Spirit. He continues to clean up our messes with his Word and presence. Nothing could be more perfect!

November 15

Major objections
Mike Novotny

The faith of countless people has been shaken, even destroyed, by the problem of pain. Here's why: In the Bible, God claims to be (1) all-knowing, (2) all-powerful, and (3) entirely good. If God is entirely good but didn't know about the abuse you endured, you couldn't blame him for not stopping it, but God did know. He is all-knowing. Or if God knew about your learning disability but didn't have the power to cure it, you couldn't be any madder at him than your mother. But God does have the power. He is all-powerful. Or if God knew and had the power but wasn't good, you would get why he'd just sit there and watch you struggle to find meaningful work, but he claims to be entirely good. The combination of those three qualities—all-knowing, all-powerful, entirely good—add up to a major objection to God's existence.

Have you thought about that tension? Have you dealt with it? In the devotions to come, I want to explore some of the most powerful answers that suffering Christians have held on to when pain shakes their faith. But for now, ponder your own answer. If someone asked you how a good God can exist in such a bad world, what would you say? When their souls are crying out, how would you respond to this: **"My God, I cry out by day, but you do not answer, by night, but I find no rest"** (Psalm 22:2)?

How do you personally deal with the problem of pain?

November 16

Finding hope
Mike Novotny

There was an old rabbi who traveled in a strange and dangerous country with only his donkey, rooster, and lamp. When he stumbled into a small village, exhausted and desperate for lodging, the villagers denied him room, forcing him to sleep in the nearby forest. The frustrated rabbi settled near a tree, where he lit his lamp to read the Scriptures, but a merciless wind snuffed out the flame. Soon after, wild animals chased his rooster away, and then a group of thieves snatched his donkey. His suffering felt unfair, unjust, pointless.

But the next morning, the rabbi wandered back into the village, where he discovered an answer to his suffering. The previous night, the village had been raided by enemy soldiers who attacked the villagers in their beds, the same soldiers who then marched by the very forest where the rabbi was sleeping. If they had seen the light of his lamp or heard the crow of his rooster or seen the shape of his donkey, he would have died. So the old rabbi sighed, "All that God does is done well."

No matter how painful your life may be or get, the moral of the rabbi's story holds true: **"In all things God works for the good of those who love him"** (Romans 8:28). Whether you see all of God's plan, catch only a glimpse of it, or can't fathom his bigger purpose, God is always using his power and love to work out pain for a greater good.

Believe that, and you will find hope in your suffering.

November 17

He gets it
Mike Novotny

I'm not very good at pastoral counseling, but I do know this: Most people are more blessed by deep empathy than by quick answers. Hurting people want a person who gets it, someone who feels with them. Logic and solutions are not bad, but they're not always the best answer to begin with.

If you're hurting today, please remember that Jesus gets it. Perhaps the most famous prophecy about Jesus, Isaiah 53, includes this: **"He was despised and rejected by mankind, a man of suffering, and familiar with pain"** (verse 3). Jesus didn't feel pain once or twice; he was "familiar with" it.

Do you come from a poor family? He gets it. Have you been misunderstood or rejected? He gets it. Have you been betrayed by a friend or hurt by the church? He gets it. Have you seen sickness and darkness up close? He gets it. Have you gone to the funeral of a friend? He gets it. Have you been verbally or physically abused? He gets it.

When you suffer, Jesus looks you in the eyes and says, "I get it. And I'm sorry. This is not how it's supposed to be. This is not how it was in the beginning. This is not how it will be one day. But this is what it is right now. I hate it, but I get it."

Is God working out your pain for a greater purpose? Absolutely. But he is also with you in the darkness, looking you in the eyes with compassion and assuring you, "I get it."

November 18

Remember your salvation
Mike Novotny

I was in an Uber as my Middle Eastern driver drove me to my hotel. "What are you here for?" he asked.

"To give a presentation on trusting God even when life hurts."

"I do trust in God like that," he declared. He then told me when Hurricane Harvey flooded his house and threatened not only his stuff but his life, even then he trusted God to do whatever was best.

"How did you get faith like that?" I asked him, curious.

That's when he told me about Afghanistan, about the day during the war when he got shot but lived due to a bulletproof vest.

"It was like someone shoved me to the ground," he said of the bullet that zipped into the vest that saved his life. And once God saved him, this man knew he could trust God.

Once God saves you, you know you can trust him. This was Paul's logic in Romans 8: **"He who did not spare his own Son, but gave him up for us all—how will he not also, along with him, graciously give us all things?"** (verse 32). In not sparing his only Son, God saved you. That's why you can trust him, even when you don't understand him.

I don't claim to understand why you have suffered in the ways you have, but I do know enough about our Savior to trust him. If Jesus died for you, then God must care. He must love you.

Remember your salvation, and you will get through this suffering.

November 19

Jesus had a job too
Ann Jahns

Have you ever noticed that we know surprisingly little about Jesus' life before he began his formal ministry around the age of 30?

Because he wasn't born into a wealthy family, we know he worked. The Bible books of Matthew and Mark refer to Jesus as a carpenter, but that word in Greek could also mean a builder, stonemason, or common craftsman. Can you imagine the Lord of the universe, who called all things into existence with his very words, sweating away in the hot sun, working with scratched and callused hands?

But it really doesn't matter exactly what Jesus did for a living, does it? What matters is this: The work Jesus did, he did faithfully and well. He did the job placed in front of him with his whole heart. Through his everyday labor, he supported his family, showed love to others, and honored his Father in heaven. He knew his work mattered.

Our work matters too. Every ungrateful customer we serve, every diaper we change, every spreadsheet we labor over matters. Even if no one seems to notice or care. God does.

The apostle Paul reminds us, **"Whatever you do, work at it with all your heart, as working for the Lord, not for human masters, since you know that you will receive an inheritance from the Lord as a reward. It is the Lord Christ you are serving"** (Colossians 3:23,24).

Jesus had a job too. Just like you. Just like me. Serve God faithfully, and for Jesus' sake, he promises to bless you for a job well done.

November 20

You can't just quit God
Jason Nelson

I know some fine Christian people who are in anguish because a child or grandchild isn't going to church. Their loved one may even express doubts or say they no longer believe. This hurts for fear they will be lost eternally. Our concern for their souls can push us to hound them about it or fill their inbox with Grace Moments devotions. But our well-meaning efforts can backfire. For the sake of bringing comfort to so many of us, I am going to overstate my case. It is not our job to hold on to God. It is his job to hold on to us. You see, no one can just quit God. He has given us this assurance: **"I'll never let you down, never walk off and leave you"** (Hebrews 13:5 MSG).

It is very difficult to just walk away from God. There may be times in people's lives when abandoning what they grew up learning about him makes their lives easier. Less internal conflict. Fewer difficult decisions. Not so much guilt. But God insists, "You're not going to just walk away from me. I will do something about it." He will not give up on anyone he has claimed as his own through Baptism or any other conversion to faith in Jesus. I promise you this. Before God quits on anyone, he will orchestrate events in their lives to produce soul searching and wondering if their lives could possibly have any meaning without him.

November 21

Resting grace face
Liz Schroeder

Today I met a lady in the checkout lane whose face positively glowed. I struck up a conversation with her and found out that she counsels veterans struggling with mental health. It was easy to see that she loves her job, loves people, and loves her Lord. You could say she has a "resting grace face."

I've been told my face has closed-captioning. Apparently, you don't need to wonder what I'm thinking; just read my face. How about you? Do you have a poker face, or are you an open book?

Proverbs tells us, **"A happy heart makes the face cheerful, but heartache crushes the spirit"** (15:13).

A patient, peaceful countenance stands out in a slow-moving store checkout. A contented heart preaches sermons in a society hell-bent on overconsumption. Your visage makes an invisible God visible. Your face shares the love of Jesus before you even open your mouth!

If God has blessed you with working eyeballs, be on the lookout for people experiencing the second half of this proverb. When you notice a neighbor heavy with heartache or a coworker with a crushed spirit, you can listen, empathize, affirm, and direct them to the source of your joy. You can lead them to Christ. On the cross, the Father turned his face away from the Son because Jesus bore our sins. He turned his face away from Jesus so that he could turn his face toward us.

May the Lord shine his face upon you today, and may your face reflect his grace to everyone God puts in your lane.

November 22

Tune your instrument
Katrina Harrmann

Have you ever started your day on the wrong foot?

Sometimes it's caused by doing things out of order.

The other day, I woke up late. And cranky. And I grabbed my coffee and hopped on social media. First thing. Yikes.

You can probably guess what kind of mood that put me in.

And my day didn't get any better.

What if I had prayed or read some Scripture or a devotion before hopping on my computer? Maybe I would have had a better attitude and a better day!

British missionary Hudson Taylor may have hit the nail on the head when he said, "Do not have your concert first, and then tune your instrument afterwards. Begin the day with the Word of God and prayer, and get first of all into harmony with Him."

Once we align ourselves with our Creator and connect with him, it can help put the rest of our day into alignment.

In Hebrew, there is a word: *Ayekah*. God asked it in the garden of Eden. It means, "Where are you?"

God always knows where we are *physically*. Rather, this word infers something deeper: "How are you? Where is your soul in relation to me?"

Every morning we can ask ourselves that. Are our internal compasses pointing toward God? Once we orient ourselves like this, we can go about our day headed in the right direction.

"Since, then, you have been raised with Christ, set your hearts on things above" (Colossians 3:1).

November 23

The burden of sin
Christine Wentzel

Have you ever caught yourself feeling the weight of church or personal rules? Traditions with no biblical basis, eating certain foods or not at certain times, or believing that if you just did life the right way God would be pleased?

Thankfully, earning God's favor has nothing to do with you: **"It is by grace you have been saved, through faith—and this is not from yourselves, it is the gift of God—not by works, so that no one can boast"** (Ephesians 2:8,9). Salvation is God's gift to you through Jesus.

The New Testament book of Galatians is a great place to start reading more about this truth. This book is a letter the apostle Paul wrote to Christians in Galatia (modern-day Turkey) to remind them of the freedom they had through the life, death, and resurrection of Jesus. At this time, there were false teachers who said Christians needed to fulfill the Jewish law of circumcision for salvation, and the Galatian Christians were confused and tempted by it. Paul showed them their salvation was all about Jesus, not about what they did. The same is true for you and me.

In our time, there are false teachings to navigate as well, but we can remember, **"It is for freedom that Christ has set us free. Stand firm, then, and do not let yourselves be burdened again by a yoke of slavery"** (Galatians 5:1).

Don't be burdened by your sin. Jesus already carried it away for you. Trust in him!

November 24

What exactly is Holy Communion?
Mike Novotny

Christians have long wrestled with what exactly Jesus meant when he said, "This is my body" and "This is my blood." Are Jesus' body and blood somehow present? Or was Jesus saying that the bread and wine symbolically represent his body and blood?

Curious for answers, I searched through the Scriptures. Here's what I found in the texts that teach us about Communion. In Matthew 26, Jesus said, **"This is my body/This is my blood."** In Mark 14, **"This is my body/This is my blood."** In Luke 22, **"This is my body/This cup is the new covenant in my blood."** And in 1 Corinthians 11, **"This is my body/This cup is the new covenant in my blood."** That's eight instances of the word *is* without any clues that Jesus was speaking in metaphors.

Now, the Bible sometimes does speak symbolically, so I looked up every passage that uses the word *symbol* (there are 13) and every passage that uses the word *represent* (there are 14) and every passage that uses the word *sign* (there are 189), but none of them are about Communion. Ever.

Perhaps this is why St. Augustine, one of the biggest theologians in Christian history, stated, "That bread which you see on the altar, having been sanctified by the word of God, is the body of Christ. That chalice, or rather, what is in that chalice, having been sanctified by the word of God, is the blood of Christ."

November 25

A prayer for patience
Jan Gompper

A friend of mine gave me a refrigerator magnet that read: *Lord, grant me patience. . . . but I want it right now!* She was friend enough to remind me humorously that I sometimes have trouble waiting for the Lord's timing.

Truthfully, there is nothing humorous about being impatient. Marshall Segal of desiringGod.org illuminates: "Impatience is a child of our pride and unbelief. It rises out of our frustration that we do not control what happens and when in our lives."*

Remember the Israelites in the wilderness? God had delivered them from slavery in Egypt and provided them with daily bread to sustain them, **"but *the people grew impatient on the way;* they spoke against God and against Moses, and said, 'Why have you brought us up out of Egypt to die in the wilderness? There is no bread! There is no water! And we detest this miserable food!'"** (Numbers 21:4,5).

"Shame on them!" we say. Now think back to our journey through COVID. Did we grumble because of the inconveniences *we* suffered? Or how about our current journey through a world riddled with wars, political tensions, and inflation? Have we, at times, thrown up our hands in despair, thinking *we* will never see better days?

If so, let's revisit the words of King David: **"Be still in the presence of the Lord, and wait patiently for him to act"** (Psalm 37:7 NLT).

Lord, grant me patience . . . to trust *your* timing!

---

* Marshall Segal, "Impatience Is a War for Control," desiringGod.org, November 12, 2021, https://www.desiringgod.org/articles/impatience-is-a-war-for-control#modal-602-rjekesui.

November 26

Sinner or saint?
Clark Schultz

Life is full of contradictions. Think of the person who races to find the closest parking spot to the doors at the gym. Couldn't the workout begin with a few extra steps? Or the person who orders the 20-piece nuggets, the large order of fries, two cherry pies, and . . . a diet soda. I'm not anti-gym or anti-diet soda. But you can see the contradictions.

You know who else is a walking contradiction? You. And me. The apostle Paul tells us in Romans 3:23: **"All have sinned."** Yes, all of us, and we don't need a trainer to show us where our spiritual muscles in giving, loving, and sharing with others are weak. At the same time, Paul says in Romans 3:24 that **"all are justified freely by his grace."** So which is it? Are we saints, or are we sinners? YES! No, I'm not doing an Abbott & Costello bit of "Who's on First?" here, but the life of a Christian can be viewed as a contradiction.

Why does it matter? Perhaps you know a friend caught in sin but ask yourself, "Who am I to say anything to him since I'm just as guilty?" You are, but like him, you are also a sinner who has been set free from the heavy weight of sin. You have been given the greatest gift ever, a guilt-free life full of God's grace.

Use your freedom to speak the truth in love to those who desperately need it.

November 27

The real city of gold
Mike Novotny

Back in the 1540s, a Spanish nobleman named Francisco Vázquez de Coronado came to Mexico City and decided that he would be the one to find the legendary Seven Golden Cities. He raised the needed funds, compiled a massive force, and set out to find paradise. After months of travel, Coronado made it to what is now the American Southwest, but instead of finding streets of gold, he discovered the Pueblo people whose homes were made of . . . mud. But a rumor reached his ears that the gold was even further north, which led Coronado hundreds more miles into modern Kansas, where he came upon villages made of . . . straw. After two years of hard travel and zero pieces of precious gold, Coronado headed home.

That adventurer never found what he was looking for, but through Jesus, you will. You will find a place more precious than gold, where every need is met, every desire is satisfied, a place where God is, where nothing bad ever happens (ever!), where the only something you experience is something so, so good. I know life can be bad. I know life sometimes gets worse. But don't worry, because Jesus wins and the new earth is on the way.

"The angel said to me, 'These words are trustworthy and true. The Lord, the God who inspires the prophets, sent his angel to show his servants the things that must soon take place'" (Revelation 22:6).

Thanksgiving Day | **November 28**

Today is a gift
Ann Jahns

On my bed sits a decorative pillow. In gold script, it elegantly declares, "Today is a gift." I treasure this pillow for two reasons: It was a gift from my youngest son, and it is a daily reminder of God's unchanging goodness.

Thanksgiving Day is a day when it's easy to remember to be grateful for God's gifts. If you are spending the day with loved ones, you may even list the ways that God has blessed you.

Yes, today is a gift from God. But what about the days that don't feel like a gift? Days when you would like to take my inspirational pillow and throw it against the wall? Like the day you get the news you've been dreading? Or the day you finally admit that your marriage is over? Or the day you are so weary—physically, emotionally, and even spiritually—that you just want to give up?

In his book, James talks about finding "pure joy" in those types of days. He reminds us, **"Every good and perfect gift is from above, coming down from the Father of the heavenly lights, who does not change like shifting shadows"** (1:17). I love that final reminder of God's immutability—he *does not change like shifting shadows.* This world offers us false, fleeting gifts. Only the gifts from our heavenly Father are perfect. And through those, he blesses us.

Today is a gift. And tomorrow. And every day that God gives us. *Lord, help us to recognize each day as the perfect gift it is. Amen.*

November 29

Spiritlink
Linda Buxa

Noland Arbaugh was 21 years old when a diving accident paralyzed him, leaving him with quadriplegia. Eight years later, he is the first person in a clinical trial to receive a brain implant by Neuralink. This Elon Musk company is designing a brain-computer interface that will collect brain signals, analyze them, and then translate those into commands that control external devices. The company wants to give more freedom and independence to those who can't move on their own.

Admittedly, I'm both fascinated and a little weirded out by a brain-computer link.

But then I realized that I'm in the same situation. Before I was baptized, I couldn't do anything on my own. But once I was baptized, I was united to Jesus' death and raised to life—and so are you.

You can read that good news in Romans 6:3-5. And then in Romans 8:10,11, Paul describes that thanks to that connection, we are now implanted with "Spiritlink": **"But if Christ is in you, then even though your body is subject to death because of sin, the Spirit gives life because of righteousness. And if the Spirit of him who raised Jesus from the dead is living in you, he who raised Christ from the dead will also give life to your mortal bodies because of his Spirit who lives in you."**

Because we have the Spirit of the Lord, we have the freedom to do all sorts of things we couldn't do before—love others, exercise patience, be faithful, practice self-control, choose gentleness, and be filled with joy and peace.

November 30

God and government
Daron Lindemann

Do you feel like the United States government could do a better job? Do you trust the president? Do you wish our nation was more patriotic? Here's what you can do.

Daniel worshiped God, even while taken captive by a foreign country. He was put to work there in the king's cabinet because he **"distinguished himself . . . by his exceptional qualities. He was trustworthy and neither corrupt nor negligent"** (Daniel 6:3,4).

Daniel courageously practiced his faith, even under a government that disagreed with his godly beliefs. He served faithfully in a pagan government.

While doing so, Daniel focused his energy less on changing his government and more on being true to God in his beliefs and behavior. It wasn't always popular. His opponents framed him and got him tossed to the lions for insubordination. But God delivered him.

"No wound was found on him, because he had trusted in his God" (Daniel 6:23). What if Daniel had trusted in government instead of God to save him?

Be careful of trusting in the government to do for you what only God can do. Be careful of trusting in government over God. God is more powerful than lions, kings, and presidents. Serve him fully and faithfully.

God, I pray for our country and that I live in it honorably as I follow you. You are sovereign over all governments. Rule my heart so that I trust you more, shining for you through my beliefs and behavior. Amen.

DECEMBER

Therefore the Lord himself will give you a sign: The virgin will conceive and give birth to a son, and will call him Immanuel.

ISAIAH 7:14

December 1

Best 1,260 days ever
Mike Novotny

The mysterious book of Revelation reveals some of God's greatest promises: **"The dragon [Satan] stood in front of the woman who was about to give birth. . . . The woman fled into the wilderness to a place prepared for her by God, where she might be taken care of for 1,260 days"** (12:4,6). 1,260 days? That's a symbolic way of saying, "God will care for us to the very end."

Here's why—1,260 days is about 42 months (30 days/month), and 42 months is 3.5 years, and 3.5 is half of 7. In the Bible, the number 7 often represents a complete period of history, like God created a 7-day week. Thus 3.5 years or 42 months or 1,260 days is the half of history from Jesus until the end of the world (from his ascension around A.D. 30 to whenever the Last Day arrives). Just like God provided for his people until Jesus came (the first 1,260 days), so he will care for us until Jesus comes again.

The Bible's closing promise is that no matter how dark these last days get, God will care for us. We might be outmatched by the power of Satan, the barrenness of this broken world, or our own unworthiness, but God has a place prepared for us where he takes perfect care of us.

Whether today is your last day or you live until the glorious return of Jesus, please remember what those 1,260 days represent. They are God's promise to get you to the finish line, where the true celebration begins.

December 2

Trust God's protection
Andrea Delwiche

Are we preoccupied with self-protection? We worry about financial self-protection and choose political candidates based on who serves our needs. Our obsessive working, careful networking, and even the slate of activities we plan for our children might all be seen as forms of protecting status and opportunities. Yet Scripture also counsels us to work diligently and care for our loved ones. What kind of balancing act is God asking of us?

Here's good counsel from Psalm 127: **"Unless the Lord builds the house, the builders labor in vain. Unless the Lord watches over the city, the guards stand watch in vain. In vain you rise early and stay up late, toiling for food to eat—for he grants sleep to those he loves"** (verses 1,2).

Our plans are nothing if they don't follow God's plan. Whatever we're striving for is chaff in the wind if humble obedience to God and his ways isn't first in our lives. God promises protection.

"Whoever claims to live in him must live as Jesus did" (1 John 2:6). Jesus lived every day of his life trusting in the protection of God his Father. Never once did Jesus justify his actions with arguments of *self*-protection.

How would the world's view of Christianity change if we all started to look and live more like Jesus? Would we have more time to protect *others* if we trusted God to protect *us*?

Meditate and pray with these words from Isaiah 30:15: **"In repentance and rest is your salvation, in quietness and trust is your strength."**

December 3

The power of example
Katrina Harrmann

We took our kids sledding several years ago at the dunes near Lake Michigan. These can be quite steep and provide some awesome opportunities for sledding!

Our nine-year-old daredevil walked up one of the tallest dunes with his older brother and plunked his sled down. He gained speed pretty fast and went flying through the air in spectacular fashion. His glasses went one way, the sled went a second way, and the small boy flew in a third direction.

I remember shrieking—I was so sure he must have broken something. He was shaken up, but he was okay.

His older brother, age 13, had watched it happen from where both boys had started out, at the top of the dune. After watching it unfold, our older son quietly descended about halfway down the dune before trying his sled out on a calmer slope—one much less likely to send him airborne.

Smart cookie! We learn by example, right?

We see others go through things, and we learn. Examples are powerful, because we see the effects of various actions taken (good and bad) in front of our eyes!

How much more so the powerful examples of our own lives?

The next time you think that leading a quiet life of Christian values isn't doing much at all, think again! Leading by example—even a quiet example—is a powerful witnessing tool!

"In everything set them an example by doing what is good" (Titus 2:7).

December 4

Satan's two biggest lies (and how to overcome them)
Mike Novotny

Satan knows that one of two lies will work with you—taking sin too lightly or taking sin too seriously.

Maybe you take sin too lightly. How often do you really feel bad for sinning? You're only human, right? At least you didn't _____, right? Some of us have so much self-compassion that we let go of the perfection.

Or maybe you take sin too seriously. You can't let it go. You can't move on. You can't forgive yourself. You don't deserve to pray (what a hypocrite you would be if you did!). You don't have a chance with God and never will. Joy is something that other people, better people, feel but not a disgusting sinner like you.

Both lies can devour your faith.

Here's the truth that triumphs over them both: **"They triumphed over [Satan] by the blood of the Lamb"** (Revelation 12:11). How can your sin not be a big deal if Jesus must bleed for it? How can you claim that your sin isn't serious when you see him suffering? Sin is bad, as bad as the bleeding Son of God.

But how can you be unforgivable if that same blood cleanses you? If the Lamb laid down his life for you, how are you not good with God? If Jesus shouted, "It is finished," how could sin and shame not be finished for you?

Meditate on the blood of the Lamb, and you will have the truth that triumphs over both of Satan's biggest lies.

December 5

The dysfunctional family tree
Ann Jahns

Anyone who writes knows that the first few sentences are critical. If you don't draw your reader in, they won't make it any further. (Are you still with me?)

Matthew starts his gospel, the first book of the New Testament, with 17 seemingly dry verses listing Jesus' family tree. This probably wasn't the "hook" his creative writing teacher was looking for.

But guided by the Holy Spirit, God inspired Matthew to write these words for a reason, and what a story they tell! After establishing that Jesus is **"the son of Abraham,"** the descendant of the revered father of the Jewish people (verse 1), Matthew throws in something unexpected.

Unlike typical genealogies of the time, Matthew includes women. Women like Tamar (verse 3), who through deceptive and sordid events became pregnant by her father-in-law, Judah. Or Rahab (verse 5), a former prostitute who became a follower of the true God. Or even Ruth (verse 5), not a native Israelite but a believer and the grandmother of the great King David.

Each ancestor in Jesus' family tree was sinfully dysfunctional—from the "good" ones, like Abraham, to the "bad" ones, like Rahab. But they also had something else in common: They were made perfect by the blood of their descendant/Savior, Jesus Christ, **"who is called the Messiah"** (verse 16).

I urge you to read Matthew 1:1-17 with fresh eyes. See the miracles in the mundane. Recognize God's grace. Marvel at how God used sinful people to advance his kingdom plan.

If God used people like these in his plan, he uses you too!

December 6

Break up the snake
Linda Buxa

Stick with me. There's a lot of backstory . . .

In 1407 B.C., the Israelites were complaining (again!)—and God sent poisonous snakes. The people *quickly* realized the consequences of their absolute disrespect and asked Moses to plead their case—and God sent a solution. Moses made a bronze snake and lifted it on a pole. When the poisonous snakes bit them, people could look at the pole and live.

In 716 B.C.—that's 700ish years later—Hezekiah became Israel's king and **"did what was right in the eyes of the Lord"** (2 Kings 18:3). He removed all the items and places associated with idol worship, which included breaking **"into pieces the bronze snake Moses had made, for up to that time the Israelites had been burning incense to it. (It was called Nehushtan.)"** (verse 4).

Instead of worshiping God for the healing of their ancestors, they had been worshiping the snake itself.

So what do we worship in place of God? Are we tempted to focus more on the answer to our prayers than we are on the Answer-er? Maybe it's our cancer-free status, the babies born after years of infertility, the exercise routine that helped with the weight loss, the homes we live in, the income from a job, the doctors who performed the surgery, possibly even the leaders whom God has put in authority over us.

Whatever it is for me and whatever it is for you, today is a good day to reflect on what we worship. If things are in the wrong order, break up the snake.

December 7

Which way to pray
Jason Nelson

I recently learned that during my long catastrophic illness, there were differences of opinion on how to pray for me. Thankfully, many people were praying for me. But as time went on and word got out that I had yet another life-threatening complication, there was a debate among folks who cared about me. Do we pray for another healing, or do we ask God to take Jason home? I was at times in the latter camp.

Miracles versus mercy. Sometimes it is a tough call, and only God can make it. Right now, it looks like he was in the let's-heal-this-guy-one-more-time camp. Thank you, Jesus. Many in my generation will pivot from prayers for miracles to live to prayers for a merciful end to it all. It would be a morbid lottery to bet on which of us goes first. But no one will escape that inevitable outcome.

Life and death are God's domain. So, we pray. What did I learn from being the subject of so many prayers? **"I know that through your prayers and God's provision of the Spirit of Jesus Christ what has happened to me will turn out for my deliverance"** (Philippians 1:19). I don't understand why I was delivered and others weren't, why I lived and others didn't. But I have resolved to be as vigorous as I am able and tell people how much I love them.

Yes, I'm ready to die. But not today.

December 8

The blessings of being a beginner
Liz Schroeder

It's difficult to start a new language at any age, but it's doubly humbling to learn one later in life. The sponge-like brain of youth has been swapped out for a bowling ball: hard and smooth, and I think there's a hole or two in there.

Because of my work with a global nonprofit, I decided to learn Indonesian. After months of daily usage of the app, I could order eggs for breakfast. How would I like them cooked? Um, yes?

I'm grateful for the experience because it reminds me what it feels like to be a beginner. It's exciting to see progress and how much I have yet to learn.

That's the feeling I get from watching my friend Lucinda grow in her faith. Lucinda will tell you that she is Navajo, a mother, a recovering alcoholic, and a child of God. Our pastor recently gave her a self-study Bible, so Lucinda and I met for coffee to crack open her new treasure.

As we read in the book of Mark about John the Baptizer and the baptism of Jesus, the dawn of realization brightened Lucinda's face. "I'd like to get baptized!" By the grace of God, Lucinda will be baptized next Sunday, just days after celebrating nine months of sobriety.

Jesus tells us in John 14:26, **"But the Advocate, the Holy Spirit, whom the Father will send in my name, will teach you all things."** Better than any app, we have the Holy Spirit to guide us in our baby steps of faith. What a blessing!

December 9

Our times, God's hands
Karen Spiegelberg

Ticktock. The hours and minutes ticked away until his alarm clock signaled it was time to get up and go to work. He had packed his lunch the night before and laid out his clothes, sure of another day ahead. But when the alarm rang, he didn't wake up. The Lord had taken my brother to heaven unexpectedly in the middle of the night.

I thought I was confident in God's promise of his perfect timing, but my brother's sudden death hit me like a ton of bricks. I wanted to question God's timing of taking him, a dad to three young kids and a blessing to our family. I bared my broken heart to God while searching his Word. When I landed on Psalm 31, I was completely taken in by King David's words and reminded of the much greater difficulties that he had encountered. But David knew that he was under the care and perfect timing of our God Almighty. When I hit verses 14 and 15, a peace washed over me: **"But I trust in you, Lord; I say, 'You are my God.' My times are in your hands."** That passage reminded me of God's daily providence while I am still awake in my time of grace.

Ticktock. All of our times are in God's hands. Our pasts are forgiven through the blood of Christ, the present is covered through his provision, and our futures are certain by his promise of eternal life!

December 10

Perhaps tithing was easier
Matt Ewart

When God rescued Abraham's descendants from Egypt and made them into a nation, he provided the laws and ceremonies by which they would operate. Among the laws was a command to tithe. The tithe required that each person give back to God ten percent of what they received.

This command enforced a life that kept God first. In fact, God specified that he wanted the first ten percent of what they got, not the leftovers. When they gave back the first portion, it forced them to remember God and rely on him for the rest.

The command to tithe is no longer in effect since it specifically applied to the people of Israel. But before you get too comfortable, Jesus replaced the tithe with an invitation to do even more: **"A new command I give you: Love one another. As I have loved you, so you must love one another"** (John 13:34).

And Paul says in Romans 12:1: **"I urge you . . . in view of God's mercy, to offer your bodies as a living sacrifice."**

Whereas Old Testament tithing enforced a life that kept God first, New Testament giving reflects the truth that God put us first. God gave all of his one and only Son to redeem us from sin and death. His love invites us to reflect a similar love, not just giving because we are commanded to do so but giving freely and giving wholly because this is now part of who we are in Christ.

December 11

Turn lemons into lemonade
Christine Wentzel

I sat in a hospital waiting room anxious to take a major heart test. This was the last place I expected to be. Shocked, frightened, and downright mad at God, I sat there stewing in misery. An older woman walked in, and our eyes met with the same knowing look of what we faced. We smiled and mumbled hellos. She asked me how I was. I told her the truth and finished with a resigned, "Whatever . . ." She replied, "We can pray," and we did.

My wise, watchful sister in Christ made lemonade out of our lemons. The taste was sweet and long lasting. She had no idea if I knew my Savior or not, but with faith in her conviction, she took advantage of a God-given opportunity anyway. She had no idea it helped place my fears at the cross of Christ and trust in him. She had no idea she was an inspiring demonstration of a gospel-motivated life.

The apostle Paul encourages us to keep praying, to be alert, and to be thankful. He assures us there will be opportunity to reveal the gospel to others. The situation will be tailor-made. Since that time in the hospital, I've also gone out on a limb of faith and prayed for and with strangers. It's not easy at first but gets better with practice. Help is here!

"But the Advocate, the Holy Spirit, whom the Father will send in my name, will teach you all things and will remind you of everything I have said to you" (John 14:26).

December 12

Giving our children to the Lord
Dave Scharf

Hannah from the Bible was barren. All she wanted in life was to have a child. If God were to bless her with a child, she vowed to give him into the Lord's service for his whole life. And the Lord answered. He gave her Samuel, who would become a great prophet in Israel's history. And then the time came for Hannah to take him to serve at the tabernacle.

Hannah said, **"So now I give him to the Lord. For his whole life he will be given over to the Lord"** (1 Samuel 1:28). He was maybe five years old. Can you imagine what it was like for Hannah? And yet, we see in the next chapter that Hannah poured out thanksgiving to God in prayer!

Could you do it? You and I are not in Hannah's situation exactly, but shouldn't we desire to give our children over to the Lord? I think of my own mother, who faithfully read devotions with us, said prayers with us, and lived Jesus for us with her forgiveness. She was intent on giving us to the Lord even after a long day. Yes, I was Mom's child, but it was more important to her that I be God's. For this, you and I will give our eternal thanks to God. If God has blessed you with a child, give that child over to the Lord. Pray with them. Read God's Word with them. Worship with them. Give them to the Lord.

December 13

How to prepare for Lord's Supper
Mike Novotny

After studying every Bible passage on the Lord's Supper, I came up with a six-part method to get the most of your next celebration of it: Look back, forward, up, down, in, and around. If you remember to look in those six directions, the Lord's Supper will be the blessing that Jesus intended.

Look back to the cross where Jesus died for you, as you **"do this in remembrance"** of your Savior (Luke 22:19).

Look forward to the feast where Jesus is waiting to eat a better meal with you **"in the kingdom of God"** (Luke 22:16).

Look up to give thanks that our God, unlike the gods of all other religions, has a **"new covenant"** where he forgives you freely (Luke 22:20).

Look down to see the gift, the true body and blood of Christ, which is present with the bread and the wine (Luke 22:19,20).

Look in to repent, ridding your heart of any **"yeast"** (sin) that might spread quickly (1 Corinthians 5:7).

Look around to rejoice, noticing all the people breaking bread with you because they share your beliefs (1 Corinthians 10:17).

Got that? Look back to the cross, forward to the feast, up to give thanks, down to see the gift, in to repent, and around to rejoice. (I'd recommend memorizing that last sentence right now.) Lord's Supper is too sacred to speed through the motions. So look back, forward, up, down, in, and around, and you will be prepared for a miracle that only Jesus can do.

December 14

Scared or prepared?
Clark Schultz

My five-year-old son came home from kindergarten saying, "I'm not scared; I'm prepared." He then went on to tell me that he practiced hiding from the wolf today in school. *Hmm.* Is this like new math (what was wrong with the old math)? Are they bringing live animals into the classroom now?

My wife and I deduced that the teacher was preparing her students for an active shooter drill. Yes, this is the world we live in, and sadly we need to teach these lessons to our children. This got me thinking about Matthew 10:28: **"Do not be afraid of those who kill the body but cannot kill the soul. Rather, be afraid of the One who can destroy both soul and body in hell."** When the end of the world or last days become a topic of discussion, what is your reaction? Are you scared or prepared?

Jesus spoke these words when he was sending out his disciples on their intern mission trips, not to be confused with the Great Commission, which came later. He was preparing his disciples, as well as preparing us. When the end comes, we DO NOT need to be scared. Why? **"Even the very hairs of your head are all numbered. So don't be afraid; you are worth more than many sparrows"** (Matthew 10:30,31).

We thank the school and teachers for their teaching and preparing our children for all situations. We thank our pastors, teachers, parents, and grandparents for showing us that ONLY JESUS can destroy the wolf.

December 15

Are you a confident Christian?
Mike Novotny

Feeling confident (a.k.a. hopeful, optimistic, etc.) comes down to a simple equation: Confidence = Resources > Needs. For example, you feel confident about passing a class when your resources (like your intelligence, your previous grades, your study habits) are greater than the needed knowledge for the class. You feel confident you can afford something (that house, that car, that phone) when your resources (savings and income) are greater than the needed price. That's the confidence equation.

Based on that definition, you, I, and every Christian can be supremely confident. Will you make it to heaven? Does God like you? Is God for you? Will he use (your learning disability/health dilemma/chronic pain) for some higher purpose? To all these questions and more, we shout, "Absolutely!" Because Jesus is always greater than any and every need.

When we have Jesus, we have the ultimate resource, a source of forgiveness, salvation, and power. Instead of looking in the mirror and trying to find enough inner resources to meet the needs of life, Jesus turns us toward the cross, where we find everything we need, freely given in his blood.

Paul wrote, **"In [Jesus] and through faith in him we may approach God with freedom and confidence"** (Ephesians 3:12). Tell your insecurity to take a hike. You have Jesus Christ, which is all you need to be a confident Christian.

December 16

God's operator's manual
Andrea Delwiche

This won't surprise you, but there's no long-lost recipe for a trouble-free life. Jesus told his followers, **"In this world you will have trouble"** (John 16:33). The sweet, untroubled face of a sleeping child stirs us in part because children are largely free from worry, including the reality that we won't be able to protect them from tears.

We persevere because we have hope in Christ. We can also *thrive* if we choose to follow the operator's manual of sorts that God laid out for us in Scripture. God's commands are *practical.* He hasn't handed down his laws and guidelines to trip us up. He has given them to provide a road map and the best preventative care manual ever printed.

"Blessed are all who fear the Lord, who walk in obedience to him. You will eat the fruit of your labor; blessing and prosperity will be yours" (Psalm 128:1,2).

This is no recipe for financial wealth or earning our way to heaven. It's a realization of the facts of existence. God created us, loves us, and knows best how, under his care and blessing, we can succeed.

"[God's] **commands are not burdensome,"** writes the apostle John in 1 John 5:3. We show love for God by obeying his commands, and then *we* are the ones who reap the benefits of living a life of love for God.

This too is part of the saving message of Jesus. We are saved for eternity, but we are also saved for a life of meaning, purpose, and joy in the here and now.

December 17

Jesus will heal you
Mike Novotny

You can't read the Bible and deny that Jesus cares about our bodies. Jesus didn't just teach; he also touched. He didn't just preach; he put his hands on sick and blind and dead bodies and gave them health, sight, and life. In fact, most of Jesus' miracles were about physical bodies that needed to be healed.

Since Jesus is the same yesterday, today, and forever, I want you to be confident that he can do the same for you. He can heal you. More than that, Jesus will heal you.

Sooner or later, Jesus will heal your body. Your migraines, arthritis, anxiety, cramps, and cancer are all like those hourglass sand timers, and every day is one day closer to your pain being gone for good. Through medicine or surgery or a miraculous snap of his fingers, either today or next year or on the day when he returns, Jesus will heal your body. Do you believe that?

The apostle Paul, who both experienced miracles and lived with an excruciating "thorn" in his flesh, confidently wrote, "[The Lord Jesus] **will transform our lowly bodies so that they will be like his glorious body**" (Philippians 3:21). Jesus *will!* Not might. Not maybe. Not depending on how he feels. No, Jesus will transform our lowly, broken bodies. We won't ache or hurt forever. One day soon, Jesus will return with power and love to transform these lowly bodies into something glorious and new.

You are one day closer to the healing you have ached for. Pray with me—Come quickly, Lord Jesus!

December 18

HELP WANTED!
Clark Schultz

Perhaps HELP WANTED signs litter the sidewalks on your daily commute. Maybe you're the one looking for help or a job.

As a teen, my parents encouraged me to find a job that paid well, and if I didn't like it, to stick with it and not quit. It's advice I pass on to this generation of "I need to find the perfect job" workers. Working at a place that is difficult gives perspective on what real work is and teaches life lessons of pain, struggle, and an appreciation for the people and the work done at the business.

When it comes to our salvation, we too need big HELP WANTED signs on our heads and hearts. By nature, our sinful condition means we should not be hired but fired into the pit of hell. But then came Jesus. **"Jesus began to explain to his disciples that he must go to Jerusalem and suffer many things . . . and that he must be killed and on the third day be raised to life"** (Matthew 16:21). Jesus took the job that we could never do. He did all the tasks the Father asked him to do, and he did them perfectly. He did not quit. In turn, he gave his life for our lives, he paid the ransom for our sins, and he gave us the paycheck of eternity.

Help wanted? Yes! Help given in Jesus! That's a sign we can proudly display!

December 19

Why religious people are afraid
Mike Novotny

The other day I asked ChatGPT why people who believe in God still become afraid. In impressive time, the artificial intelligence typed out a list of answers that I, as a Christian, found fascinating. Reason #1: "People may fear the unknown, death, or the afterlife." Reason #2: "Religious individuals often adhere to a set of moral and ethical principles outlined by their faith. Fear of deviating from these principles or facing divine judgment for perceived wrongdoing can contribute to anxiety or fear." Catch that? The top reasons for fear are uncertainty about the afterlife and being judged for our sins.

I wonder who could help with that (insert knowing smile here)? Speaking of Jesus, the apostle Paul declares, **"He was delivered over to death for our sins and was raised to life for our justification"** (Romans 4:25). If Jesus died for our sins, then we don't need to fear God judging us for our wrongs. We are completely forgiven for every time we have deviated from the moral principles outlined by Jesus. And if Jesus rose to life, then we know precisely what happens after death. We open our eyes to see the perfect face of our forgiving Father in heaven.

Friend, too many people forget the fear-erasing power of the cross and the empty tomb. Today, I urge you to remember Jesus. Your fear doesn't stand a chance next to him!

December 20

JOY.
Katrina Harrmann

I sat in my living room after having a rough day. I was surrounded by twinkle lights and listening to Christmas music, just getting a chance to relax. I glanced down at my cocoa mug and saw the word inscribed on it—JOY.

I laughed at the period. It wasn't JOY! It was JOY. Period.

JOY. is very different than JOY!

JOY. is a call to action. An imperative.

As I held that mug, the music I was listening to wailed about glad tidings of great joy, and I thought about how for many people, joy doesn't come in an obvious way, like the shepherds—their quiet night rent with angel fire, the heavenly shrapnel of which literally smacked them upside their heads. (That was JOY!)

For many people, JOY of any kind is an effort.

For families dealing with sickness or loss . . . or joblessness or strain . . . no JOY! For people who are emotionally strained . . . no JOY!

But, perhaps, still . . . JOY.

If we choose to hunt it down like the wise men, dedicated and curious and longing for that speck of light . . . JOY.

A search. A command.

A baby in a manger.

Who gives JOY. to countless without JOY!

"Consider it pure joy, my brothers and sisters, whenever you face trials of many kinds, because you know that the testing of your faith produces perseverance" (James 1:2,3).

December 21

We are prayer warriors
Christine Wentzel

I confess that in the past, when I read on social media that someone needed a "prayer warrior" to pray for their health or loved one or struggle, my first thought was, "That counts me out."

For years I struggled with my prayer life. To tell someone I would pray for them often meant I would save it until I could do it privately if I remembered. I rarely prayed on the spot, let alone face-to-face with that person.

"I'll pray for you" has become a cliché to the world and even in some Christian circles because it is either taken as a platitude that people just say but don't mean or with skepticism—especially if it's not backed up with actions such as actual prayer and then follow-up to see how the person is doing.

I've learned to push past my fears of not having the right words to say or even believing the lie that my prayers are too little for God to bother with. How did I do that? I remembered what God says about my prayers.

He says, **"Therefore confess your sins to each other and pray for each other so that you may be healed. The prayer of a righteous person is powerful and effective."** (James 5:16).

God promises my prayers and yours are powerful and effective! Improving our prayer lives is an ongoing process. We can't let our fears of messing up or feeling self-conscious prevent a chance to open a door to the power of God. We ARE prayer warriors!

December 22

A God with skin on
Jan Gompper

A visiting pastor at church told the story of a little girl who cried out in fear after having a bad dream. Her mother rushed to comfort her, assuring her that God was with her and that he would take care of her. To the mother's surprise, her daughter replied, "I know that God is with me, Mommy, and that he'll take care of me, but I want somebody here with skin on."

Have you ever wanted "a God with skin on"? Maybe you wished you could've held Jesus' hand physically from your hospital bed. Perhaps you ached for a hug from Jesus when you learned of the death of a loved one or when your spouse wanted a divorce. Though we know God is with us, sometimes a God with skin on would help, wouldn't it?

The disciples *did* experience a God with skin on, yet they still had doubts and fears, even after hearing of Jesus' resurrection. While they huddled behind closed doors, Jesus appeared to them, saying, **"Why are you troubled, and why do doubts rise in your minds? Look at my hands and my feet. It is I myself! Touch me and see; a ghost does not have flesh and bones, as you see I have"** (Luke 24:38,39).

How do people experience a God with skin on today? **"Now *you* are the body of Christ, and each one is a part of it"** (1 Corinthians 12:27). So whenever you bring a word or touch of comfort to hurting or frightened souls, they see and feel Jesus.

December 23

Storing up
Linda Buxa

"Mary treasured up all these things and pondered them in her heart" (Luke 2:19).

When I'm feeling ungrateful about my blessings, I think about my grandma. I go to bed with the dishwasher running. She washed dishes by hand. My laundry is washed and dried after a few pushes of buttons. She washed hers by hand and hung them on a clothesline. I can drive to the store, and in minutes my freezers and refrigerators (note the plural) are full. She stockpiled her abundance by canning and storing the vegetables from her garden. She knew she needed to store up when there was an abundance so the family would have provisions when conditions weren't as favorable.

The same is true for our faith. Mary treasured up—stored up, canned up—all the moments of Jesus' life, including when the shepherds visited her baby and the wise men later brought him gifts. Then when a sword was piercing her soul because a sword was piercing his side, she could go back to those stored-up moments and know he was fulfilling his mission.

Your stored-up provisions might not be as dramatic, but they are just as important.

When life is good, store up the goodness of God in your heart. When you feel his peace, can it in the jars of your heart so that when life hurts—and it will—you can go back to that abundance and know that he has provided in the past, provides in the present, and will provide in the future.

December 24 | Christmas Eve

Right-on-time delivery
Liz Schroeder

As a kid, I remember Christmas gift labels that read, "Do not open until December 25." Oh, the thrill of anticipation that coursed through my eight-year-old body! What could be under the wrapping? And please, God, let it be the stuffed unicorn I circled in the Sears catalog!

When God promised Adam and Eve that a Savior would be born, they didn't understand God's timeline. He didn't tell them when they could open the gift, only that the Gift would come. So when Eve became pregnant, she assumed her baby was the Messiah. In truth, she gave birth to Cain, who would grow up to become a murderer (see Genesis 4).

If God had put a gift label on the promised Messiah, it would have read, "Do not open for four thousand years." That's a long time to sustain anticipation!

"But when the set time had fully come, God sent his Son, born of a woman, born under the law, to redeem those under the law, that we might receive adoption to sonship" (Galatians 4:4,5).

As a parent, it's hard for me to wait until Christmas to give our kids their gifts. When it's the perfect gift, I can't contain my excitement. I wonder if that's a taste of how my heavenly Father felt during those four thousand years?

God has a Christmas gift for you: an adoption certificate signed in the blood of his Son. Go ahead and rip off the wrapping. His forgiveness, love, and acceptance are yours to enjoy right now.

Christmas Day | **December 25**

Decorations doing their job
Daron Lindemann

What are your Christmas decorations telling you?

The evergreen tree. The glistening lights. The nativity scene. It is all symbolism that helps you celebrate. Just like the number of candles on a birthday cake symbolizes your age.

Typically, however, symbolism tends to lose its meaning over time, and the symbol becomes the thing instead of pointing to the thing. Like when Christmas dinner makes everybody so stressed out that they forget about the peace of Jesus.

The Bible reports an epic event as the Israelites crossed the Jordan River and entered their new land. To commemorate the event, God commanded Joshua to set up 12 stones at their camp. He wanted that pile of stones to be a reminder in the future. He wanted the Israelites to ask, **"What do these stones mean?"** (Joshua 4:21).

Take an inventory of your Christmas decorations and ask, "What does this mean?" Do this as you take down the decorations. Write down notes for next Christmas, perhaps doing this same exercise as you take the decorations out of the box and display them next year. Teach your children.

The evergreen Christmas tree symbolizes everlasting life, and it points up like an arrow to heaven. The candy cane represents Jesus, white because he is holy with red stripes for the blood he shed to save us. Wrapped gifts remind us that God wrapped himself in flesh and became the gift of salvation for sinners. And more!

Do some research about the symbolism of Christmas, and help your decorations do their job.

December 26

God's positive thinking
Dave Scharf

Positive thinking can sometimes just be pretending. The philosophy of "Ignore a problem, and it will go away" or "It's only a problem if you treat it like one" sounds comical until the sad reality dawns on you that this is the approach to spiritual needs for many.

The apostle Paul said, **"Finally, brothers and sisters, whatever is true, whatever is noble, whatever is right, whatever is pure, whatever is lovely, whatever is admirable—if anything is excellent or praiseworthy—think about such things"** (Philippians 4:8). Notice what the first qualification for positive thoughts is: They have to be true.

This is the truth: I am a great sinner, but I have a greater Savior in Jesus, who died and rose for me. He won for me forgiveness and a guaranteed life in heaven! Now I wake up every day as a forgiven child of God, knowing that my Jesus is with me, he loves me, he is guiding all things for my good, he is blessing my life beyond what I can possibly imagine, he is preparing a mansion for me in heaven, he has freed me to give him glory in my life and in countless ways to thank him for his goodness to me, and I have all I need in him. The next time you start thinking negatively, ask yourself who is the epitome of everything Paul lists in this verse? It's Jesus. That is true positive thinking!

December 27

The story ends (kind of) like it began
Mike Novotny

The final chapter of the Bible says, **"Then the angel showed me the river of the water of life, as clear as crystal, flowing from the throne of God and of the Lamb down the middle of the great street of the city. On each side of the river stood the tree of life, bearing twelve crops of fruit, yielding its fruit every month. And the leaves of the tree are for the healing of the nations. No longer will there be any curse"** (Revelation 22:1-3). Sound familiar?

Back in the beginning, there was a *river* that flowed from Eden. And there was *fruit* and *the tree of life* and people who walked with *God*. The Bible's final verses are meant to take us back to the original world before the curse of sin corrupted it.

Except this version of paradise is even better, an upgraded Eden. Because the devil doesn't slither in this garden (he was tossed into the lake of fire in Revelation 20) and God promises, "No longer will there be any curse." Never again will work hurt or marriage be messy. Never again will we sin or feel shame or hide from God.

Your story, because of Jesus, ends with all blessing and no curse, a new kind of Eden. Except this paradise will not end in a page or two. It will endure forever.

Today you are one day closer to what the Bible's final pages promise. Hold on tight, child of God. You are so close to experiencing what Adam and Eve did, only better!

December 28

Are you good enough for God?
Mike Novotny

Recently, my friend went to a funeral of a man who was dearly loved by his community because he had served his community deeply. But during the service, the priest admitted that the deceased had not been confident he could make it to heaven. Was he good enough? Had he done enough good? The priest went on to say, "The saints in heaven are those who do good on Earth."

Let's think about that for a second. How good is good enough to be with God? It takes a lot to get into Harvard, and heaven is way better than Harvard, so what spiritual test score is required? You can try your best, but is your best enough for God? (And how often do you actually try your best?) No wonder so many people are not confident they are going to heaven.

Forgive me for judging another man's funeral sermon, but that priest was wrong. You don't get to God by being good. None of us are good enough. I'm not. You aren't either.

But Jesus is. Paul's words on this subject are classic for a reason: **"For it is by grace you have been saved, through faith—and this is not from yourselves, it is the gift of God—not by works, so that no one can boast"** (Ephesians 2:8,9). Salvation is all about God's grace, about faith in Jesus, about the gift the Lord gives when he declares, "I forgive you at the cross!"

Believe in Jesus. He is all you need to be good enough for God.

December 29

How can I know God's will?
Daron Lindemann

A man hiking at night fell off a cliff. He managed to grab a branch that stopped him from tumbling to his death. But he knew he wouldn't be able to hold on for long. He called out, "Is anyone up there?"

After what seemed like an eternity of silence, he heard God's response, "I can help."

The man eagerly waited for his miraculous deliverance. "Let go of the branch!" God commanded.

The man questioned why God would tell him to do something so foolish. This wasn't deliverance at all. There had to be a better option. "Is anyone else up there?" the man inquired. All the while, as he dangled from the branch, his feet were only six inches off the ground.

We often wish that we knew more about God's will. We pray and struggle trying to figure out the right way. All the while, however, God has clearly revealed his will to us. Printed plainly in the Bible.

Jesus once said, **"My Father's will is that everyone who looks to the Son and believes in him will have eternal life"** (John 6:40). The apostle Paul wrote, **"We instructed you how to live in order to please God. . . . It is God's will that you should be sanctified"** (1 Thessalonians 4:1,3).

The Bible gives us God's perfect promises to live by and God's guidance to make life even better. What would change in your life if you started paying more attention to God's will that he already reveals?

December 30

Piercing wisdom
Matt Trotter

"Then Simeon blessed them and said to Mary, his mother: 'This child is destined to cause the falling and rising of many in Israel, and to be a sign that will be spoken against, so that the thoughts of many hearts will be revealed. And a sword will pierce your own soul too'" (Luke 2:34,35).

Have you wondered what to say to someone who's grieving? It's hard to muster more than, "I'm sorry." And that's okay; expressing sorrow is a good thing. Even though Mary knew what the future held for her Son, she felt sorry too.

It was not until the tragic death of my daughter that the pointedness of the sword Simeon wrote of stung me. When my daughter had her last MRI, I could see it in the faces of the nurses and staff as a sharp pain started in my chest. It felt like panic and dread, like a heart attack—but it was my soul being pierced.

Losing a child is a piercing of a parent's soul. It's a scar that never fully goes away. When people ask me what it felt like to lose a child, I say, "It still feels as if a pen was stuck into my chest." It still hurts. I think of this more as I age and realize other people are wounded in this way too.

Next time you meet someone in grief, think no further than Mary, the mother of Jesus, a perfect Son, and yet her soul was pierced. It's okay to be sorrow-full, to be sorry.

December 31

Abide
Katrina Harrmann

At the close of every year, I like to pick out a word for my coming year.

I enjoy this more than trying to decide on a resolution for the year because, let's face it, resolutions are easy to make but pretty hard to stick to.

Instead, if I choose a word, I can often think about it and pray over it and ruminate about what it means in my life.

This past year, my word was *Abide*.

We happened to be singing a song in church at the close of last year, and the lyrics talked about asking God to teach us to abide.

I love the idea of abiding. Of "learning" to abide.

It doesn't mean that life is perfect.

It means that I am learning to "BE" where God has placed me.

It means that I am learning to lean into him . . . depend on him.

This was a great thought for me to bring to mind during high and low moments of the year.

Consider choosing a word that means something to you and that you think you'd enjoy holding close or considering! Words like *faith, trust, patience,* and *joy* are good places to start. Or choose an entire Bible verse that you can bring to mind throughout the year!

"Abide in me, and I in you. As the branch cannot bear fruit by itself, unless it abides in the vine, neither can you, unless you abide in me" (John 15:4 ESV).

About the Writers

Pastor Mike Novotny pours his Jesus-based joy into his ministry as a pastor at The CORE (Appleton, Wisconsin) and as the lead speaker for Time of Grace, a global media ministry that points people to Jesus through television, print, and digital resources. Unafraid to bring grace and truth to the toughest topics of our time, he has written numerous books, including *3 Words That Will Change Your Life*, *When Life Hurts*, *Lonely Less*, and *Taboo: Topics Christians Should Be Talking About but Don't*. Mike lives with his wife, Kim, and their two daughters, Brooklyn and Maya; runs long distances; and plays soccer with other middle-aged men whose best days are long behind them. To find more books by Pastor Mike, go to timeofgrace.store.

Linda Buxa is a freelance communications professional as well as a regular blogger and contributing writer for Time of Grace Ministry. Linda is the author of *Dig In! Family Devotions to Feed Your Faith*, *Parenting by Prayer*, *Made for Friendship*, *Visible Faith*, and *How to Fight Anxiety With Joy*. She and her husband, Greg, have lived in Alaska, Washington D.C., and California. After Greg retired from the military, they moved to Wisconsin, where they settled on 11.7 acres and now keep track of chickens, multiple cats, and 1 black Lab. Their 3 children insisted on getting older and exploring what God has planned for their lives, so Greg and Linda are now empty nesters. The sign in her kitchen sums up their lives: "You call it chaos; we call it family."

Andrea Delwiche lives in Wisconsin with her husband, three kids, dog, cat, and a goldfish pond full of fish. She enjoys reading, knitting, and road-tripping with her family. Although a lifelong believer, she began to come into a deeper understanding of what it means to follow Christ far into adulthood (always a beginner on that journey!). Andrea has facilitated a Christian discussion group for women at her church for many years and recently published a book of poetry—*The Book of Burning Questions*.

Pastor Matt Ewart and his wife, Amy, have been blessed with three children who keep life interesting. Matt is currently a pastor in Lakeville, Minnesota, and has previously served as a pastor in Colorado and Arizona.

Jan Gompper spent most of her career teaching theatre at Wisconsin Lutheran College in Milwaukee. She also served six years as a cohost for *Time of Grace* during its start-up years. She has collaborated on two faith-based musicals, numerous Christian songs, and has written and codirected scripts for a Christian video series. She and her husband now reside in the Tampa area, where she continues to practice her acting craft and coach aspiring acting students as opportunities arise. She also assists with Sunday school and other church-related activities.

Katrina Harrmann lives in southwest Michigan with her photographer husband, Nathan, and their three kids. A lifelong Christian, she attended journalism school at the University of Missouri, Columbia, and worked at the *Green Bay Press-Gazette* and the *Sheboygan Press* before taking on the full-time job of motherhood. Currently, she is an editor for Whirlpool and lives along the shores of Lake Michigan and enjoys gardening, hiking, camping, doing puzzles, and playing with her chihuahua in her free time.

Ann Jahns and her husband live in Wisconsin as empty nesters, having had the joy of raising three boys to adulthood. She is a marketing coordinator for a Christian church body and a freelance proofreader and copy editor. Ann has been privileged to teach Sunday school and lead Bible studies for women of all ages. One of her passions is supporting women in the "sandwich generation" as they experience the unique joys and challenges of raising children while supporting aging parents.

Pastor Daron Lindemann loves the journey—exploring God's paths in life with his wife or discovering even more about Jesus and the Bible. He serves as a pastor in Pflugerville, Texas, with a passion for life-changing faith and for smoking brisket.

Jason Nelson had a career as a teacher, counselor, and leader. He has a bachelor's degree in education, did graduate work in theology, and has a master's degree in counseling psychology. After his career ended in disabling back pain, he wrote the book *Miserable Joy: Chronic Pain in My Christian Life*. He has written and spoken extensively on a variety of topics related to the Christian life. Jason has been a contributing writer for Time of Grace since 2010. He has authored many Grace Moments devotions and several books. Jason lives with his wife, Nancy, in Wisconsin.

Pastor Dave Scharf served as a pastor in Greenville, Wisconsin, and now serves as a professor of theology at Martin Luther College in Minnesota. He has presented at numerous leadership, outreach, and missionary conferences across the country. He is a contributing writer for Time of Grace and a speaker for Grace Talks video devotions. Dave and his wife have six children.

Liz Schroeder is a Resilient Recovery coach, a ministry that allows her to go into sober living homes and share the love and hope of Jesus with men and women recently out of rehab or prison. It has been a dream of hers to write Grace Moments, a resource she has used for years in homeschooling her five children. After going on a mission trip to Malawi through an organization called Kingdom Workers, she now serves on its U.S. board of directors. She and her husband, John, are privileged to live in Phoenix and call CrossWalk their church home.

Pastor Clark Schultz loves Jesus; his wife, Kristin, and their three boys; the Green Bay Packers; Milwaukee Brewers; Wisconsin Badgers; and—of course—Batman. His ministry stops are all in Wisconsin and include a vicar year in Green Bay, tutoring and recruiting for Christian ministry at a high school in Watertown, teacher/coach at a Christian high school in Lake Mills, and a pastor in Cedar Grove. He currently serves as a pastor in West Bend and is the author of the book *5-Minute Bible Studies: For Teens*. Pastor Clark's favorite quote is, "Find something you love to do and you will never work a day in your life."

Karen Spiegelberg lives in Wisconsin with her husband, Jim. She has three married daughters, six grandchildren, and has been a foster mom to many. Years ago she was encouraged to start a women's ministry but was unsure of the timing. When her brother died suddenly, it hit her hard—that we can't wait until the time seems right for our ministry; the time is now. And so in 2009, with God's direction, A Word for Women was born. Karen finds great comfort in Psalm 31:14,15: "But I trust in you, O Lord. . . . My times are in your hands."

Matt Trotter is the president and CEO of Time of Grace Ministry. His responsibilities include ensuring the ministry stays true to its vision/mission, overseeing the business aspects of the ministry, shaping the strategic direction, and creating a culture in the organization that makes it the "best job ever" for every employee. Matt and his wife, MJ, have been blessed with five daughters of resplendent beauty and boundless energy. Together the family enjoys school, volleyball, swimming, and training their faithful dog, Mars.

Christine Wentzel, a native of Milwaukee, lives in Norfolk, Virginia, with her husband, James, and their rescue dogs. After two lost decades as a prodigal, Christine gratefully worships and serves at Resurrection Lutheran in Chesapeake, Virginia. In 2009 she served as writer and coadministrator for an online Christian women's ministry, A Word for Women. In 2022 she accepted a position to become the social media director for the WELS military ministry that sees to the spiritual needs of active duty members serving in the armed forces.

About Time of Grace

The mission of Time of Grace is to point people to what matters most: Jesus. Using a variety of media (television, podcasts, print publications, and digital), Time of Grace teaches tough topics in an approachable and relatable way, accessible in multiple languages, making the Bible clear and understandable for those who need encouragement in their walks of faith and for those who don't yet know Jesus at all.

To discover more, please visit **timeofgrace.org** or call **800.661.3311.**

Help share God's message of grace!

Every gift you give helps Time of Grace reach people around the world with the good news of Jesus. Your generosity and prayer support take the gospel of grace to others through our ministry outreach and help them experience a satisfied life as they see God all around them.

Give today at timeofgrace.org/give or by calling 800.661.3311.

Thank you!

TIME OF GRACE